福建省文化和旅游厅 策划
资源开发处 组织编写

编著
宋春

翻译
[美]Richard Howe
黄兆儒

摄影
郑友裕
宋春 等

福建的世界遗产

World Heritage Sites in Fujian

武夷山
Mount Wuyi

海峡出版发行集团
THE STRAITS PUBLISHING & DISTRIBUTING GROUP

福建人民出版社
FUJIAN PEOPLE'S PUBLISHING HOUSE

图书在版编目（CIP）数据

武夷山：汉英对照 / 宋春编著；（美）豪子（Richard Howe），黄兆儒译 . --福州：福建人民出版社，2020.5（2021.10 重印）
（福建的世界遗产）
ISBN 978-7-211-08314-5

Ⅰ.①武… Ⅱ.①宋… ②豪… ③黄… Ⅲ.①武夷山—介绍—汉、英 Ⅳ.①K928.3

中国版本图书馆 CIP 数据核字（2019）第 288379 号

武夷山
WUYISHAN

作　　者：宋　春	
翻　　译：〔美〕Richard Howe　黄兆儒	
责任编辑：孙　颖	
美术编辑：陈培亮	
装帧设计：〔澳〕Harry Wang	
内文排版：良之文化传媒	
出版发行：福建人民出版社	电　　话：0591-87533169（发行部）
网　　址：http://www.fjpph.com	电子邮箱：fjpph7211@126.com
地　　址：福州市东水路 76 号	邮政编码：350001
经　　销：福建新华发行（集团）有限责任公司	
印　　刷：雅昌文化（集团）有限公司	
地　　址：深圳市南山区深云路 19 号	
开　　本：787 毫米×1092 毫米　　1/16	
印　　张：17.25	
字　　数：382 千字	
版　　次：2020 年 5 月第 1 版	
印　　次：2021 年 10 月第 2 次印刷	
书　　号：ISBN 978-7-211-08314-5	
定　　价：88.00 元	

目 录

Contents

01

世遗档案

UNESCO's Introduction to Mount Wuyi

◎ 武夷山水。（彭善安 摄）
The landscape of Mount Wuyi. (Photo by Peng Shan'an)

名　　称：**武夷山**
列入时间：1999年12月
遗产类型：世界文化与自然遗产

　　武夷山脉是中国东南部最负盛名的生物多样性保护区，也是大量古代孑遗物种的避难所，其中许多生物为中国所特有。九曲溪两岸峡谷秀美，寺院庙宇众多，虽然其中不少早已成为废墟，但曾为唐宋理学的发展和传播提供了良好的环境。自11世纪以来，理学对东亚地区的文化产生了相当深刻的影响。公元前2世纪时，汉朝统治者在武夷山附近的城村建立了一处较大的行政首府，厚重坚实的围墙环绕四周，极具考古价值。

◎ 武夷仙境。（晏音 摄）
A fairyland—Mount Wuyi.
(Photo by Yan Yin)

Mount Wuyi

Inscribed on the World Heritage List in 1999
World cultural and natural property

Mount Wuyi is the most outstanding area for biodiversity conservation in southeast China and a refuge for a large number of ancient, relict species, many of which endemic to China. The serene beauty of the dramatic gorges of Nine-Bend Stream, with its numerous temples and monasteries, many now in ruins, provided the setting for the development and spread of Neo-Confucianism, which has been influential in the cultures of East Asia since the 11th century. In the 2nd century BCE a large administrative capital was built at nearby Chengcun by the Han Dynasty rulers. Its massive walls enclose an archaeological site of great significance.

遗产价值

位于中国东南部省份福建的武夷山拥有中国最大、最具代表性、保留最为完整的森林，体现着中亚热带森林和中国南部雨林的生物多样性。就保护生物多样性的重大意义而言，该处遗产是众多古代孑遗植物的避难所，其中许多生物为中国所特有，且拥有极其丰富的动植物，包括数量众多的爬行、两栖和昆虫动物种类。

九曲溪两岸峡谷险峻，颇具宁静之美，光滑的岩石峭壁峭立于清澈幽深的溪水之上，独具韵味。九曲溪沿岸庙宇众多，虽然多数已成废墟，但曾为自11世纪以来在东亚地区影响深远的政治哲学思想——理学的发展与传播提供了良好的环境。尤其值得一提的是，武夷山分布着不少于35家古代儒学书院，其历史始于北宋，绵延至清代。此外，武夷山还可以看到墓葬、题刻和藏着历史可以追溯至商代的木质船棺的岩穴，以及60多座道教寺观遗迹。

◎ 九曲溪之美。（郑友裕 摄）

The beauty of Nine-Bend Stream. (Photo by Zheng Youyu)

◎ 欢歌。（朱庆福 摄）
Birds singing happily. (Photo by Zhu Qingfu)

Outstanding Universal Value

Mount Wuyi, located in China's southeast province of Fujian, boasts the largest, most representative example of a largely intact forest encompassing the diversity of the mid-subtropical forest and the rainforest in southern China. Of enormous importance for biodiversity conservation, the property acts as a refuge for an important number of ancient, relict plant species, many of which endemic to China, and contains extremely rich flora and fauna, including significant numbers of reptile, amphibian and insect species.

◎ 猴群。（郑友裕 摄）

A troop of monkeys. (Photo by Zheng Youyu)

The serene beauty of the dramatic gorges of Nine-Bend Stream is of exceptional scenic quality in its juxtaposition of smooth rock cliffs with clear, deep water. Along this river are numerous temples and monasteries, many now in ruins, which provided the setting for the development and spread of Neo-Confucianism, a political philosophy which has been very influential in the cultures of East Asia since the 11th century. In particular there are no fewer than 35 ancient Confucian academies dating from the Northern Song to Qing dynasties (10th to 19th centuries). In addition, the area boasts tombs, inscriptions and rock shelters with wooden boat-shaped coffins dating back to the Shang Dynasty (over 3,000 years ago), and the remains of more than 60 Taoist temples and monasteries.

公元前2世纪，汉代统治者在武夷山城村附近建立大型行政首府，其巨大的城墙包围起一个具有重要意义的考古遗址。

武夷山世界文化与自然遗产包含四个区域：位于西部的武夷山国家级自然保护区、位于中部的九曲溪生态保护区、位于东部的武夷山国家级风景名胜区和独矗于东南方向15千米以外的古汉城遗址保护区。武夷山世界文化与自然遗产总占地面积1070.44平方千米，被占地面积为401.7平方千米的缓冲地带环绕，因其文化、风光及生物多样性价值而被联合国教科文组织纳入《世界遗产名录》。

◆ 武夷山是一处被保护了超过1,200年的美丽景观。它拥有一系列特殊的考古遗址，包括建于公元前2世纪的汉城遗址、大量的寺庙以及与诞生于公元11世纪的朱子理学相关的书院。

◆ 武夷山是朱子理学的摇篮。朱子理学曾在东亚和东南亚国家中占据统治地位长达数百年，并影响了世界上不少地区的哲学思想和政治统治。

◆ 九曲溪（下峡谷）风景区东部的壮观地貌成就了其非凡景色，红色砂岩构成的巨石绝壁陡然而立，形成九曲溪长达10千米的天际线。它们以200—400米之高度耸峙于河床之上，底部深藏于清澈幽深的河水之中。这些古老崖壁上的山径不可错过，沿其登临峰顶，游客便可以鸟瞰九曲风光。

◆ 武夷山是世界上价值最突出的亚热带森林之一。它是最大的、最具代表性的、很大程度上堪称完整的中国亚热带森林和中国南部雨林，有着丰富的植物多样性。武夷山也是大量的古代孑遗植物的避难所，其中许多物种是中国所特有，且在中国其他地方很少见到。武夷山也有突出的动物多样性，特别是爬行动物、两栖动物和昆虫物种。

In the 2nd century BCE a large administrative capital was built at nearby Chengcun by the Han Dynasty rulers. Its massive walls enclose an archaeological site of great significance.

The property consists of four protected areas: Wuyishan National Nature Reserve in the west, Nine-Bend Stream Ecological Protection Area in the centre and Wuyishan National Scenic Area in the east, the three of which are contiguous, while the Protection Area for the Remains of the Ancient Han City is a separate area, about 15km to the southeast. Totalling 107,044 hectare, the property is surrounded by a buffer zone of 40,170 hectare and has been inscribed for cultural as well as scenic and biodiversity values.

◆ Mount Wuyi is a landscape of great beauty that has been protected for more than twelve centuries. It contains a series of exceptional archaeological sites, including the Han City established in the 2nd century BCE and a number of temples and study centers associated with the birth of Neo-Confucianism in the 11th century CE.

◆ Mount Wuyi was the cradle of Neo-Confucianism, a doctrine that played a dominant role in the countries of Eastern and South-Eastern Asia for many centuries and influenced philosophy and governance over much of the world.

◆ The spectacular landforms in the eastern scenic area around Nine-Bend Stream (lower gorge) are of exceptional scenic quality, with isolated, sheer-sided monoliths of the local red sandstone. They dominate the skyline for a tortuous 10km section of the river, standing 200—400 meters above the riverbed, and terminate in clear, deep water. The ancient cliff tracks are an important dimension of the site, allowing the visitors to get a bird's-eye view of the river.

◆ Mount Wuyi is one of the most outstanding subtropical forests in the world. It is the largest, most representative example of a largely intact forest encompassing the diversity of the Chinese subtropical forest and the south Chinese rainforest, with high plant diversity. It acts as a refuge for a large number of ancient, relict plant species, many of which endemic to China and rare elsewhere in the country. It also has an outstanding faunal diversity, especially with respect to its reptile, amphibian and insect species.

◎ 武夷山世界遗产证书。（阮雪清 摄）

The certificate issued to Mount Wuyi by the World Heritage Committee. (Photo by Ruan Xueqing)

From the translator: If you haven't heard of Zhu Xi, let me briefly introduce him. After Confucius and Mencius, he was one of the most famous and influential Confucian scholars in Chinese history. It was his writings during the Song Dynasty that served as the standard examination texts for scholars for over 600 years. Zhu Xi spent much of his life in Mount Wuyi area, studying, writing, teaching and relaxing in several cottages near the stream. Suffice it to say, he was one of the world's greatest philosophers and his works changed the culture of China from the Song Dynasty to the present day.

Prior to the Song Dynasty, China had three main philosophies: The earliest was Daoism, then Confucianism, and then Buddhism entered China. After the initial establishment of these philosophies, they all broke off into many different schools—each one interpreting the founder's teachings in their own divergent ways, but each claiming to follow the one true "Truth". Zhu Xi's genius was in recognizing and then synthesizing all these divergent views into one all-pervasive Chinese philosophy, called "Daoxue", the teaching of the way, ... Even though there were many scholars who preceded him, his synthesis was ingenious. Zhu's insight was first to realize that all these ancient philosophies were saying essentially the same thing—just in different ways; and then to redefine them with his special Song Dynasty Chinese characteristics.

Regarding this book (or any good book), Zhu Xi had this to say,

"Reading a book means investigating it for its true meaning."

And to help guide you, he added, "If one keeps a relaxed mind in reading a book, the true meaning, will, of itself, come to dawn on one."

This latter concept is more deceptive than it looks; he is saying, "Yes you must seek for the truth, but you will never 'find' it—rather it will find you on its own."

Everyone is different—that is why no one doctrine can ever be written for self-realization—likewise this book, this journey down Nine-Bend Stream will be different to every person who reads it and who travels down Nine-Bend Stream. It can be a pleasurable scenic journey through the beautiful landscapes, or it can be much more. I would humbly suggest that you "see without seeing" and "hear without hearing" ... the non-physical parts of the journey ... see the things that are not there, see/ hear/ feel with your original heart-mind, and follow the pathless pathway of the immortals.

Be like a child and just wonder—see each new mountain differently. Just empty your mind and feel ... feel nature, this omnipresent borderless entity. Don't use your senses. Just sense the unknown within the beauty. All the mountains are not the same. Look for "your" mountain, your bend in the stream, your special temple or spiritual spot.

O2

武夷大美

Mount Wuyi: A Gallery of Grand Beauty

◎ 武夷碧水丹山。（文脉 供图）

The jade waters and red mountains in Mount Wuyi. (Courtesy of Wenmai)

风景之美

碧水丹山　九曲清音

> 武夷古洞天，奇峰三十六。
> 一溪贯群山，清浅萦九曲。
> 溪边列岩岫，倒影浸寒绿。

　　宋朝名相李纲的这首诗形象地描述了武夷山国家级风景名胜区碧水丹山、九曲清音的诗意画卷。

　　九曲溪是发源于武夷山脉主峰——黄岗山西南麓的溪流，澄澈清莹，经星村镇由西向东穿过武夷山国家级风景名胜区，盈盈一水，折为九曲，因此得名。

　　九曲溪全长约9.5千米，面积约8.5平方千米。山挟水转，水绕山行，每一曲都是景致不同的山水画卷。

◎ 武夷山脉主峰——黄岗山。（郑友裕 摄）
Mount Huanggang—The main peak of Wuyi mountains. (Photo by Zheng Youyu)

The Beauty of the Landscape

Jade Waters and Red Mountains, the Soundless Rippling of Nine-Bend Stream Through the Wuyi Mountains—an Endless Beauty

"Wuyi ancient caves, thirty-six fantastic peaks,

A clear stream snaking through the mountains, haunting in nine bends;

Rocks embracing the flow, reflecting the universe in cold green."

The famous Song Dynasty (960—1279) prime minister, Li Gang, wrote this poem vividly describing the clear jade waters of Nine-Bend Stream and red mountains in Wuyishan National Scenic Area, which read like a poetic picture scroll.

Nine-Bend Stream originates from the main peak of Wuyi mountains—at the southwest slope of Mount Huanggang; its clear waters drift through ancient Xingcun Township, flowing from west to east through Wuyishan National Scenic Area around nine bends, hence the name.

Nine-Bend Stream is about 9.5 kilometers in length, with a land area of 8.5 square kilometers. The mountain carries the water and the water wraps its way around the foothills, and each bend of the stream displays a different scenic beauty as in Li Gang's poem.

From the translator: About this time some language "expert" will take issue with my choice of words. They remind me of the so-called "wine experts" at wine tasting who strut about expounding their erudite mundane knowledge—my advice to novice wine drinkers is just to enjoy the wine; my advice to readers of the book is just to enjoy the journey. Even Hui Neng, one of the greatest Chan (Zen) Buddhist masters could not read or write yet he understood the underlying meaning of the sutras, and the mysteries of the universe.

朱熹的《九曲棹歌》是历代文人赞颂武夷山的诗作中最早完整描绘九曲溪风貌的长卷佳作，九曲溪也因此歌名扬天下。

九曲棹歌

淳熙甲辰仲春，精舍闲居，戏作武夷棹歌十首，呈诸同游，相与一笑。

武夷山上有仙灵，山下寒流曲曲清；

欲识个中奇绝处，棹歌闲听两三声。

一曲溪边上钓船，幔亭峰影蘸晴川；

虹桥一断无消息，万壑千岩锁翠烟。

二曲亭亭玉女峰，插花临水为谁容；

道人不复阳台梦，兴入前山翠几重。

三曲君看架壑船，不知停棹几何年；

桑田海水今如许，泡沫风灯敢自怜。

四曲东西两石岩，岩花垂露碧㲲毵；

金鸡叫罢无人见，月满空山水满潭。

五曲山高云气深，长时烟雨暗平林；

林间有客无人识，欸乃声中万古心。

六曲苍屏绕碧湾，茅茨终日掩柴关；

客来倚棹岩花落，猿鸟不惊春意闲。

七曲移船上碧滩，隐屏仙掌更回看；

却怜昨夜峰头雨，添得飞泉几道寒。

八曲风烟势欲开，鼓楼岩下水潆洄；

莫言此处无佳景，自是游人不上来。

九曲将穷眼豁然，桑麻雨露见平川；

渔郎更觅桃源路，除是人间别有天。

◎ 九曲溪竹筏。（郑友裕 摄）

The bamboo raft on Nine-Bend Stream. (Photo by Zheng Youyu)

Zhu Xi was a famous Neo-Confucian philosopher, who wrote the *Nine-Bend Rowing Song*. It is the earliest long-volume masterpiece of that literary format from the ancient dynasties with a complete description of Nine-Bend Stream. Nine-Bend Stream is famous throughout many parts of the world just because of this poem.

The *Nine-Bend Rowing Song* was written during the middle of spring at one of Zhu Xi's leisure cottages within the Wuyi Mountains; it has 10 stanzas, and Zhu Xi often recited it to friends who traveled with him. We will use it as a guide as we float down the stream. His words are like the stream, beautiful along the surface and profound underneath.

Prelude

In the Wuyi Mountains you can still find the immortals.

Just look below the mountains in the cold current

Where the water is very clean.

And to find all the wonderful places the immortals tread …,

Just listen to Zhu Xi's rowing song

And enjoy the pathless journey down the stream with nine bends.

◎ 竹筏上的外国游客。（郑友裕 摄）
Foreign tourists on a bamboo raft. (Photo by Zheng Youyu)

　　九曲溪的次序是逆流而数，每曲之间没有明显的分界处。一般以晴川一带为一曲，浴香潭以北为二曲，电磕滩上下为三曲，卧龙潭至古锥滩为四曲，平林渡为五曲，老鸦滩为六曲，獭控滩以下为七曲，芙蓉滩东南为八曲，过浅滩为九曲。

　　武夷山国家级风景名胜区的大部分景点都分布在这一水九湾的两岸，"武夷看山不用杖而用舟"，坐竹筏游九曲，方能览其全貌胜景。古人游九曲溪，是从武夷宫按曲序逆流而上。今人则是从九曲到一曲顺流而下，所乘竹筏由8至9根去皮毛竹烤后扎成，吃水浅、浮力大，人坐在上面安稳舒适，视野开阔，观山景，赏水色，顺流而下，疾徐相间，轻松惬意。

　　著名的绘画理论家俞剑华在《武夷九曲纪游》里评价武夷九曲："九溪十八涧不及他雄秀，雁荡斤竹涧不及他悠闲，钓台七里泷不及他奇突，伦敦的康桥不及他清幽。"

　　就让我们伴着朱熹的《九曲棹歌》，与山水共鸣吧。

From the translator: Just skim over the Chinese names/ words you find difficult—some have no meaning, or it was lost eons ago, so don't get hung up on them. But there's something which I must explain. In Zhu Xi's time, people rowed UP the stream (against the current—mostly because the town was downstream). But this causes some problems for the modern travelers using the *Nine-Bend Rowing Song* as a guide. The song (and this translation) goes upstream, following the ancient route (1 to 2 to 3 to 4 ...), whereas modern travelers actually start at the ninth bend and float downstream. So if you want to use this part as a guide as you float down the stream—turn to the ninth section first, then 8, then 7, etc. Understand? I hope so. Now, let's follow the ancient travelers UP the stream.

◎ 舟行水上。（郑友裕 摄）

Drifting on the stream. (Photo by Zheng Youyu)

The flow of Nine-Bend Stream has no obvious boundaries between each turn. Generally, the area of Qingchuan is the first turn, north of Yuxiang Pool is the second turn, Dianke Shoal is the third turn, from Wolong Pool to Guzhui Shoal is the fourth turn, Pinglin Ferry is the fifth turn, Laoya Shoal is the sixth turn, Takong Shoal is the seventh turn, southeast of Furong Shoal is the eighth turn, and Guoqian Shoal is the ninth turn. Like a snake.

The scenic spots of Wuyishan National Scenic Area are distributed on both sides of the stream and eddies—even below the waters and above the mountains ... if you look with your heart and see without seeing. You can see the mountains by hiking but it's easier on a bamboo raft, drifting at times, rowing at times, through all nine turns. Ancient people traveled Nine-Bend Stream going upstream from Wuyi Palace. Nowadays people travel downstream, on shallow-draft bamboo rafts, so people can sit safely and comfortably, enjoying a wide field of vision ... watching clouds rise above majestic mountain scenery, marveling at the clear water, lazily floating downstream—the perfect environment to ponder the deeper meanings of life.

A famous Chinese art theorist, Yu Jianhua, wrote an evaluation of Nine-Bend Stream in his travel notes. He gave several examples of famous places, e.g. Hangzhou's Nine Creeks and Eighteen Gullies, Yandang's Jinzhu Stream, the fishing platform at Qililong and even Cambridge in England—and in his view none of these other places could match the sheer beauty of Nine-Bend Stream.

So as we float down, let's follow the poem by Zhu Xi and resonate with the landscape, nature and ... the beyond.

From the translator: When you look in the clear stream, notice different things ... the reflection of the mountains ... hmmm which is real, the reflection (this reality we live in) or the actual mountain (the universal, hidden original reality)? Or notice that when the stream is tranquil and clear, you can see through to the bottom. Likewise, when your own stream of thoughts of your heart-mind is calm, it's easier to "see", to understand what you cannot ordinarily see.

When I was younger, I wanted to climb every mountain—to conquer them—but often when I got to the top I only saw the tops of other mountains. Now I prefer sitting on the raft and seeing the entire mountain.

© 九曲溪风光。（郑友裕 摄）
The picturesque Nine-Bend Stream. (Photo by Zheng Youyu)

一曲

一曲溪边上钓船，

幔亭峰影蘸晴川；

虹桥一断无消息，

万壑千岩锁翠烟。

■ 幔亭峰

　　舟行一曲，见一峰巨大如翠屏，即是幔亭峰。南宋诗人辛弃疾在《游武夷·作棹歌呈晦翁十首》中赞叹幔亭峰："山上风吹笙鹤声，山前人望翠云屏。蓬莱枉觅瑶池路，不道人间有幔亭。"

　　幔亭峰的侧面峰影挺秀，正面岩壁却是肥而平。峰的半壁平坦处有勒岩擘窠大字"幔亭"，为明代吴思学所书，数里之外，清晰可见。人若站立于字下，颇觉渺小。

◎ 幔亭峰。（宋春 摄）

Manting Peak. (Photo by Song Chun)

First Bend

Get aboard the fishing boat by the first bend,

Manting Peak's shadow reflects in Qingchuan.

What news after the Rainbow Bridge broke,

Millennia of mountains and valleys hold the emerald mist.

▓ Manting Peak

Floating on the raft through the first turn, you'll see a huge peak like a giant vertical jade green screen, and that is Manting Peak. The Southern Song Dynasty poet Xin Qiji wrote a poem to praise it:

The wind blowing on the mountain,

With the calls of immortals' mounts, the crane,

People gaze at the clouds before the jade screen.

It's in vain to find the road to Yaochi in Penglai (a fabled abode of immortals)

But there is Manting Peak on earth.

The side face of Manting Peak is tall and straight, whereas the front palisade is wide and flat. On the flat half wall of the peak, there is a large inscription, "Manting", which was written by Wu Sixue in the Ming Dynasty—which you can see from far away. A person feels insignificant when he stands under these giant words … like in the nave of a very tall Medieval cathedral.

From the translator：Before we start our journey, I would like to make a personal statement, as the translator, not the Chinese author. I have traveled the world extensively, even 20 years in China, and Wuyishan National Scenic Area is truly one of my favorite places because it is uniquely special and significant on many levels: its beautiful mountains, streams and flora are a natural paradise; its historic villages honor China's glorious past; and as the cradle of Neo-Confucianism, it is a keystone to understanding Chinese philosophy and culture! Nine-Bend Stream, let's go!

《幔亭招宴》的神话故事流传已久。宋朝祝穆的《方舆胜览·建宁府卷》中记载："秦始皇二年八月十五日，武夷君与皇太姥、魏王子骞辈置酒会乡人于峰顶，召男女二千余人，虹桥跨空，鱼贯而上。设绥屋幔亭可数百间，饰以明珠宝玉……酒数行命歌师彭令昭唱人间可哀之曲。曲云：'天上人间兮会何稀，日落西山兮夕鸟飞，百年一瞬兮事与愿违，天宫咫尺兮恨不相随……'既下山，风雨暴至，虹桥飞断，回顾山顶，寂无一物。"

乡人借虹桥跨空上天，仙凡共聚，而后雨断虹桥，仙凡两分，云烟笼罩万壑千岩。

◎ 镌刻着《幔亭招宴》故事的石碑。（宋春 摄）
A stela engraved with the story of "The Manting Banquet". (Photo by Song Chun)

There is a local myth titled *The Manting Banquet* which has been passed down since ancient times. It is recorded in *The records of Mount Wuyi*, written by Zhu Mu in the Song Dynasty:

"On the 15th day of the 8th lunar month in 220 BCE, Lord Wuyi, Emperor Taimu and Ziqian (Emperor Wei) brought the villagers to the reception hall at the summit; they invited more than 2,000 men and women, and had them cross over a Rainbow Bridge, one after another. Available for them were hundreds of beautiful curtained pavilions, decorated with treasures of pearl and jade …

"After they had consumed a lot of wine, the singing master, Peng Lingzhao, sang a mourning song about life:

"When will heaven and earth be in harmony,

With the sun setting on the west side of the mountain

And the birds flying in the sky;

A hundred years is gone in one moment

But things happen not as we wish,

Heaven is here in front of our eyes

But we are sad that we can't stay …"

When they all came down from the mountain, a storm arose. Looking back at the top, they saw nothing was there. Even the Rainbow Bridge had been blown away.

From the translator: If you've read ancient Buddhist texts, you would understand what Zhu Mu was describing. For those readers less familiar, let me explain. Buddhism at this time described two ways (vessels) that seekers could use to travel across to the "other shore" (enlightenment). One was the large vessel, reciting/learning the many sutras—reading, reading, absolution, etc., the other one advocated by Hui Neng and later Chan and Zen masters was called "instantaneous" (the smaller faster boat).

In actuality, even the "instantaneous" awakening usually occurred only after many years of studying the sutras ... but that's not the point here. The point is that whichever boat they used, when they got to the other shore and looked back to where they came from (this reality)—there was nothing there! Ha! Think about that for a few thousand years.

It's really all so simple once you attain enlightenment but impossible to share—because each person, each pathway is different. That's why there has never been a "doctrine" to achieve enlightenment.

■ 大王峰

在幔亭峰南麓有大王峰，峰形如官帽，顶大腰小，上丰下敛，屹立云表，独具王者威仪，所以也被称为纱帽岩、天柱峰。大王峰矗立于九曲溪口，是进入武夷山国家级风景名胜区的第一峰，与马可·波罗齐名的"东方游圣"、明代地理学家和旅行家徐霞客游武夷就是从此处入山。如今在大王峰峰麓立有"徐霞客入山处"的牌坊和徐霞客的汉白玉雕像，游客也可自此处登临大王峰，追寻古人足迹。

古人登大王峰，旅程奇险无比，据说得架梯三重方可登顶。大王峰四周都是悬崖峭壁，只在南壁有一条狭小的孔道可供人登临峰巅。这是一条直上直下的裂罅，宽仅尺许，中凿石级，盘旋而上。裂罅越高路越窄，有的地方需侧身收腹、手脚并用才能通过。徐霞客称其为"武夷三大险径之一"。如今，裂罅间修上了水泥阶梯，蹬道共有台阶1,713级，游人可以轻松安全地抵达绝顶。

■ Great King Peak

To the south of Manting Peak there is Great King Peak. The shape of the peak is like an ancient official's hat, with a big top and a narrow waistband. Rising through the clouds, it imposes a regal vision on the surrounding area. People also call it Gauze Cap Rock or Sky Pillar Peak. Great King Peak stands at the entrance of Nine-Bend Stream. It is the first peak you see as you enter Wuyishan National Scenic Area, and the famous Ming Dynasty geographer and traveler, Xu Xiake, sometimes called the "Oriental Marco Polo", started his travel from here into the mountains when he came to Wuyi. Today there is a monument which has on it "the place where Xu Xiake went into the mountains" and a white marble statue of him at the foot of Great King Peak. Tourists can also start from here to climb the Great King Peak and follow in the ancient traveler's footsteps.

When the ancients climbed Great King Peak, the risk was much greater, as they had to use three ladders to reach the top. Great King Peak is surrounded by cliffs, and there's only a narrow path on the south palisade for people to climb to the peak. It's a straight-up crack about a foot wide, with stone steps hewn in the rock, which spirals upward and upward. The taller the crack, the narrower the pathway. In some places, people have to turn on their sides to slide through and use their hands and feet to continue. Xu Xiake called it "one of the three most dangerous paths in Wuyi". Now a cement staircase has been built in the crack, with 1,713 steps, allowing visitors to reach the summit more easily and safely. (And completely out of breath.)

● 大王峰晚照。（郑友裕 摄）
Great King Peak bathing in the evening glow. (Photo by Zheng Youyu.)

◎ 站在大王峰峰顶俯瞰群山。（陈美中 摄）
Overlooking the mountains on Great King Peak. (Photo by Chen Meizhong)

　　峰腰南壁有张仙岩，岩势险峻，相传汉代张垓曾在此修炼成仙。再向上，有天鉴池，池有流泉——寒碧泉，池侧为宋代羽士结庐修行地。从这里再升一梯，有升真观故址。从故址左侧拾级而上，则为通天台。通天台为一方巨石，登此可远眺狮子峰、兜鍪峰、虎啸岩、凌霄峰、玉女峰、观音岩等。再往上登数十米，便可抵达大王峰巅，这里地势平旷，古树参天，积叶遍地。

　　东壁岩罅间有升真洞，洞内有虹板桥跨空，船棺架临其上，历经数千年而不朽。山顶另有一岩罅，宽度一米左右，下窥黢黑，不见深浅。宋代朝廷曾多次遣使来此，投送金龙玉简，以祈国运昌盛，皇族兴旺，故名投龙洞。山顶上还有清庚子年（1900）崇安南门潘氏建立的云屏山房遗址。

　　站在大王峰峰顶俯瞰群峰碧水，山岳吞烟，玉带潆洄，美不胜收。

　　大王峰的人文景观也是一大特色。相传曾有魏王子骞等十三位武夷仙人辟谷于此，有胡、李和两鱼氏仙姑在这里修炼，故为道教圣地；又有数位高士归隐，遁入林泉，皆建庐于此处。

On the south mountainside stands Immortal Zhang's Rock, which is very precipitous. According to legend, in the Han Dynasty, Zhang Gai came here to practice becoming immortal. Then up higher, there is Tianjian Pool, where there is a spring, Hanbi Spring, and along the side of the pool there is an open area where the Song Dynasty Taoist priests practiced. Climbing a ladder again from here, you can see the old site of Shengzhen Temple. Walking further up from the left side of the site, you will see Tongtian (To the Sky) Platform. Tongtian Platform is a huge rock, and you can climb on it to overlook many mountain peaks: Lion Peak, Douao Peak, Tiger Roaring Rock, Lingxiao (Reaching the Cloud) Peak, Jade Maiden Peak, Guanyin Rock and so on. You can even go further up the peak if you climb several meters higher. The terrain there is flat with towering ancient trees and their leaves are everywhere.

Shengzhen Cave is set in the east crack rock. Inside the cave there are plank bridges (wood planks set in the rocks used as a stairway) on which the boat-shaped coffins were placed—everlasting after thousands of years. There is another crack on the top of the mountain, the width of which is about a meter, and it is very dark when you look down inside—so dark that you can't see the bottom. For many times the Song imperial court sent envoys to cast Jinlong Yujian (Gold Dragon and Jade Slip) into it to pray for the prosperity of the country and also for the royalty (a kind of Taoist ceremony). It was thus named "Casting Dragon Cave". On the top of the mountain is also the site of Yunping Mountain Study built by a man surnamed Pan in 1900.

Standing on the top of Great King Peak, overlooking the mountains and jade waters, the mountains seem to be swallowed in the mist, with Nine-Bend Stream swirling around them like a jade belt. So beautiful!

The cultural history of Great King Peak is also of major interest. Legend has it that thirteen immortals of Wuyi, including Ziqian (Emperor Wei), once fasted here (today most scientists agree that fasting and a low body weight help a person live longer), and immortals such as Hu, Li and Yu (famous Taoist masters) practiced here, making it a special sacred place of Taoism. A number of senior scholars and hermits also built their homes here and retreated into the forest and springs.

From the translator: Retreating into the mountains was a favorite Taoist pastime. The conundrum is: once you achieve self-realization, then what? Many Taoist masters saw the corrupted world and retreated to the purity of the mountain forests. Others, like Confucius and Zhu Xi, chose a different path—to try to help society.

◎ 位于大王峰下的止止庵。（郑友裕 摄）

Zhizhi Monastery under Great King Peak. (Photo by Zheng Youyu.)

■ 止止庵

　　说到武夷山的道教圣所，位于一曲的止止庵不可不提。止止庵背倚幔亭峰，左为大王峰，右有铁板嶂，三面皆穹壁，溪涧会于其前，不深而幽，不高而敞，是涵养性情的好地方。

　　相传这里是皇太姥和武夷十三仙人中的张湛及女仙鱼道超、鱼道远结庐修道之所。晋代曾有名道接踵来此，炼气养真。南宋嘉定九年（1216），名士詹琰夫出重资在此修建庵堂，以"止止庵"命名，取的是"止其所止，止观止念"之义，并延请道门高士白玉蟾到此任住持。白玉蟾撰有《武夷重建止止庵记》，其中这样描述止止庵："云寒玉洞，烟锁琼林。紫桧封丹，清泉浣玉。铁笛一声，群仙交集。螺杯三饮，步虚泠泠。青草青，百鸟吟。亦可棋，亦可琴。有酒可对景，无诗自吟心。神仙渺茫在何许？盖武夷千崖万壑之奇，莫止止庵若也。"

Zhizhi Monastery

When one talks about Taoist sanctuaries of Mount Wuyi, Zhizhi Monastery is one of the most often mentioned. Zhizhi Monastery lies in front of Manting Peak; on the left side is Great King Peak; on the right side is Tieban Mountain—three sides are all sheer vertical cliffs. Nine-Bend Stream is in front of it—not deep but secluded, not high but open … an excellent place for the cultivation of one's spirit.

Legend has it that this is the place where Emperor Taimu and some of the thirteen Wuyi immortals, Zhang Zhan, and the female immortals, Yu Daochao and Yu Daoyuan, built cottages and practiced. Some famous sages from the Jin Dynasty (265—420) followed one another to come here to refresh their spirit and cultivate the Truth. In 1216, a famous scholar, Zhan Yanfu, spent a fortune building a monastery here and called it Zhizhi Monastery. The meaning of "Zhizhi" is "stop seeing and thinking". And he invited a Taoist master, Bai Yuchan, to be the abbot. Bai Yuchan wrote *The Reconstruction of Zhizhi Monastery*, in which he described Zhizhi Monastery as follows:

> *Cold clouds and jade caves, mist wraps the beautiful forest.*
> *There are some purple junipers; buddhist ritual instruments are washed in the clear spring.*
> *A group of fairies gather together when they hear the iron whistle.*
> *Over whorl-cup drinks, they step into the cold emptiness.*
> *Green grass, birds singing, you can play chess, or music.*
> *Wine toasts to the scenery; if there is no poetry, they will sing from the heart.*
> *Where are the immortals?*
> *There are a thousand rarities in Wuyi, and Zhizhi Monastery boasts them all.*

◎ 止止庵侧影。（郑友裕 摄）
A profile of Zhizhi Monastery.
(Photo by Zheng Youyu)

◎ 止止庵门口的石狮。（宋春 摄）
The stone lion at the gate of Zhizhi Monastery. (Photo by Song Chun)

止止庵的自然环境绝佳，又曾有高士驻足，因此风流相继，屡有道众居此。

止止庵岩壁上有止止洞，好似嵌进岩壁里的一个修炼之所，洞门上勒刻"止止壶天"四字。这样一处峰岩环抱的山间谷地，精致而神秘，你若置身其中，便会自然而然地屏气凝神，静思"止其所止"之奥义。

尤为值得一提的是，止止庵有老梅数株，冬日梅开，暗香浮动。若能赶上，细嗅梅香，身心舒爽。

Zhizhi Monastery's natural environment is excellent, and many ancient scholars stopped there—hmmm … what was it like back then?

Zhizhi Monastery also has Zhizhi Cave with four characters "Zhizhi Hutian" at the entrance—like a practice hall embedded in the cliff (a great place to channel Bodhidharma). What an incredibly beautiful mountain valley! Surrounded by peaks and rocks … so delicate and mysterious. Ask these tall sentinels your unspoken questions. If you are in it, you will naturally control your breath and meditate on the meaning of "stop seeing and thinking" or as Zhu Xi put it, "quietly sitting".

What is also worth mentioning is that in Zhizhi Monastery there are several old winter plums, and when they blossom in winter, an intense fragrance floats over the area. If you can come here at this time, the sweet smell of plum blossoms will comfort your body and mind and spirit.

◎ 止止庵探梅。（宋春 摄）
The old winter plums in Zhizhi Monastery.
(Photo by Song Chun)

止止庵门前有水光石，又名晴川石，在溪北临水而立，高约数丈，每每朝晖夕照，曲水波光便映射在岩石之上，故得"水光石"之名。古时，这里是水光渡渡口，溪南溪北的游客辐辏于此，留下摩崖石刻共30余方，其文情趣各异，内涵深广。"水光""九曲溪""一曲"等题刻景名；"名山大川""引人入胜""山水奇观""万丈丹青""渐入佳景"等赞叹美景；"修身为本""智动仁静""鸢飞鱼跃""兴来独往"等格物致知；抗倭名将戚继光到此游览时也是豪兴大发，写下："大丈夫既南靖岛蛮，便当北平劲敌，黄冠布袍，再期游此。"

　　其中王守礼题著的"渐入佳景"四字，是描述此处风光的点睛之笔。

◎ 水光石。（郑友裕 摄）
Shuiguang Stone. (Photo by Zheng Youyu)

◎ 一曲风光。（郑友裕 摄）

The scenery at the first bend. (Photo by Zheng Youyu)

In front of Zhizhi Monastery, there is Shuiguang (Water Reflecting) Stone, also known as Qingchuan Stone, which stands to the north of the stream, up a few feet. During sunrise and sunset, the light reflects off the waves from the stream and glimmers on this rock—that's how it got its name. In ancient times, there was Shuiguang Ferry here. Tourists from the south and north of the stream converged here, leaving cliff inscriptions on more than 30 places. All of them express different feelings, with profound meanings (ancient philosophical graffiti): "Shuiguang", "Jiuqu Stream" and "First Bend" are names of the place; "Famous mountains and great rivers", "Fascinating scenery" and "Gradually entering the beautiful scenery" comment on the landscapes; "Self-cultivation first", "Wisdom and benevolence", "Hawks fly and fish leap" and "Come here alone" are about learning things by experiences. Qi Jiguang, one of the greatest generals fighting against Japanese pirates, was also very enthusiastic when he visited here. He wrote, "The real man needs to fight with the enemy. After that, I expect to come here again wearing yellow hats and robes (ancient robes of valor)."

"Gradually entering the beautiful scenery" is the famous line to describe the scenery written by Wang Shouli. What did he mean? "Gradually entering"? Think about it. Like entering a stream without creating a ripple. Zhu Xi, when teaching "gradually entering" had another meaning, more spiritual … later.

◎ 武夷宫。（郑友裕 摄）
Wuyi Palace. (Photo by Zheng Youyu)

一曲岸边还有几处可供悠闲踱步之处：宋街、武夷宫、万春园、柳永纪念馆等。武夷宫里有两株树龄超过900岁的宋桂，每逢中秋时节，桂花绽放，香气弥漫，坐在树下，沐浴在花香里，仿佛能与时光对话。武夷山人柳永是北宋著名的婉约词派代表人物，一生放荡不羁，热爱自由，善写儿女之情、离别之绪。他写的《雨霖铃》是一首中国大多数的孩子都背诵过的词，如今也镌刻在纪念馆祠堂后壁的墙上。

出柳永纪念馆，迎面有一书写着"渐入佳境"的牌坊，上有福建籍书法家潘主兰题写的楹联，赞叹武夷之美："如此名山宜第几，相当曲水本无多。"沿牌坊前的石阶走下去，站在一曲溪边，用旁观者的角度看竹筏上的游客，又是另外一番体验。若逢傍晚时分，光影里的景色微妙氤氲，令人沉浸忘我。

如此名山，相当曲水，为这渐入佳境的一曲做了完美的诠释。

There are several places for leisurely strolling along the shore: Song Street, Wuyi Palace, Wanchun Garden, Liu Yong Memorial Hall, and more. In Wuyi Palace there are two Osmanthus trees that are from the Song Dynasty—each one more than 900 years old. Every Mid-Autumn festival, Osmanthus blossom aromas fill the air. Time drifts away as you sit under such a tree, bathed in floral aromas. Liu Yong, a representative of the graceful and restrained school of Song Ci Poems from Mount Wuyi, was a dissolute and freedom-loving writer. He was good at dealing with romantic love or parting sorrow and wrote the famous *Yu Lin Ling*, a lyrical poem which can be recited by most Chinese children. It is engraved on the back wall of the memorial hall.

Walking out of the Memorial Hall, there is an archway with the inscription, "Gradually entering the beautiful scenery". There are also couplets written by Pan Zhulan, a famous calligrapher from Fujian Province, praising the beauty of Wuyi. Then walking down the stone steps in front of the archway, standing by the stream, looking out at the tourists on glide by rafts (from the perspective of a "watcher") is another interesting visual and spiritual experience. Every evening, the scenery of colors and light and shade change to create subtle deep, immersive feelings.

The First Bend makes a perfect introduction for a beautiful journey to such a famous mountain and stream.

◎ 柳永纪念馆。（宋春 摄）
Liu Yong Memorial Hall. (Photo by Song Chun)

◎ 二曲秋色。（郑友裕 摄）

The second bend in autumn. (Photo by Zheng Youyu)

二曲

二曲亭亭玉女峰，

插花临水为谁容；

道人不复阳台梦，

兴入前山翠几重。

Second Bend

Yunv Peak is like a slim graceful jade maiden

Standing at the second bend.

Who is she getting dolled up for

Wearing flowers and waiting beside the water?

Taoists don't dream about dating a maiden,

They just go into the green mountains.

◎ 雪后玉女更妖娆。（郑友裕 摄）
Enchanting Jade Maiden Peak after snow. (Photo by Zheng Youyu)

◎ "镜台"摩崖石刻。（郑友裕 摄）
The cliff inscription "Makeup Mirror".
(Photo by Zheng Youyu)

■ 玉女峰

　　在二曲的溪口处，有一组山峰挺立，远远地望过去，峰影倒映在水里，绰约多姿。诸峰中最为峭拔的一座俨然一位秀丽绝伦的少女，峰顶上参簇生长的花草树木好似她头上的云鬟雾鬓，而后面相伴的诸峰则如同仕女随行。古人诗里写道："玉女亭亭拥翠鬟，此心如雪照清湾。"这便是武夷山鼎鼎大名的玉女峰。

　　玉女峰的峰峦半壁有建筑残垣，留下了先民活动的踪迹。站在遗址上望向九曲溪，果真有"雨看诸曲涨，云望四山封"的开阔感。

　　玉女峰侧有一岩石，叫妆镜台，崖壁上勒有明代石刻"镜台"，"分明玉女镜中容"描述的就是这里的景致。

Jade Maiden Peak

At the mouth of the second bend, there is a group of peaks standing upright as though they are looking in the distance for their master or possibly at their reflections in the water. The most prominent one is like a beautiful emerald green maiden, with a cluster growth of flowers, shrubs and trees on the peak resembling her topknot hair with the other mountains behind her as her maidservants. The ancient poem said: "The graceful girl is surrounded by green maids, and her heart is shining on the clear bay." This is the famous Jade Maiden Peak in Mount Wuyi.

On the hillside of Jade Maiden Peak there are remnants of buildings, with traces of the activities of the ancients. Standing on the site looking out to Nine-Bend Stream, one gets closer to the saying, "See the mist rise when it rains, and the mountains wrapped by the clouds".

There is a rock on the side of Jade Maiden Peak, which is called Zhuangjing (Makeup Mirror) Platform, and there is a Ming Dynasty stone inscription for it on the cliff wall. "The maidens putting on their makeup in the mirror" vividly describes the scene here.

◎ 插花临水为谁容？（郑友裕 摄）
Who is she getting dressed up for? (Photo by Zheng Youyu)

在二曲的尽头，溪水有一个直角弯，水缓平而深，倒映着玉女峰的倩影，宛如玉女临水梳妆，这一湾碧水也因此得名浴香潭。潭中有半插入水中的岩石，方正如印章的就叫印石，形状像梳子的就叫香梳石，零星点缀在溪水之间。这些石头的名称和那玉女与大王的传说一样，带着人间烟火气，平实而亲切。从古至今，这里的景致与传说令多少才子感慨万千，作家刘白羽就曾在《武夷颂》一文里写道：

"……（玉女峰）它不但婀娜多姿，而且神情飘逸，当我们的竹筏已浮游而进，我还屡屡回顾，它使我想到我在巴黎罗浮宫中默默观赏维纳斯那一时刻我心中所升起的亲切、喜悦，完善的人和生命自由的庄严的向往。"

但喜人间烟火气呐。

At the end of the second bend, there is a right-angled bay, where the water is slow, flat and deep, reflecting the maidens dressing in front of their mirror. That is why this bay is named Yuxiang (Fragrant Shower) Pool. There are rocks halfway into the water here, dotted sporadically along the stream. One is called Yin (Seal) Stone, which looks like an ancient seal. Another is called Xiangshu (Fragrant Comb) Stone, which looks like ladies' comb. The names of these stones are similar to the legend about "Maiden and King", which comments on the meaning of man's life—plain and genial, relaxed and benevolent. From ancient times to now, the scenery and legends envelop visitors with deep emotions. Writer Liu Baiyu once wrote in *Ode to Wuyi*:

"… (Jade Maiden Peak) It was graceful and elegant. Even after my raft had passed by, I looked back at it again and again. It reminds me of the tenderness and joy that I felt when I silently looked at Venus (in the Louvre Museum in Paris), feeling the solemn yearning for perfection and freedom of people to enjoy a good life."

Be happy with this earthly life.

© 玉女峰倒影。（郑友裕 摄）
Jade Maiden Peak and her reflection. (Photo by Zheng Youyu)

◎ 小藏峰上的虹桥板。（郑友裕 摄）
The Plank Bridge on Xiaozang Peak. (Photo by Zheng Youyu)

三曲

三曲君看架壑船，

不知停棹几何年；

桑田海水今如许，

泡沫风灯敢自怜。

■ 虹桥板和架壑船

　　三曲溪南，小藏峰巍然屹立，峰岩东侧的绝壁上，几块虹桥板纵横交错地架设于岩隙之间，两具古越人架壑船搁置于虹桥板上，半插于岩隙之中，半悬于空中。小藏峰北侧半壁有石穴，名曰飞仙台，穴中有一船棺，相传内藏魏王子骞等十三位仙人的蜕骨。临近的另一个小洞穴也有虹桥板纵横架插。岩下有学者吴震文题写的摩崖石刻"架壑船"三个字。

　　武夷山至今仍保留着不少"千古之谜"，其中最著名的就包括虹桥板与架壑船。武夷山各峰的岩罅有不少木板纵横插于岩际，乡人称之为仙人桥板或虹桥板。架壑船又称仙船、仙舟，即悬于峭壁之上的船棺。它们主要分布于九曲溪沿岸和山北，位于30至50米高的悬崖绝壁，利用自然岩洞和裂隙，或置于洞内，或半插半悬空，以虹桥板作为支撑。因年代久远，自然腐蚀，现存的架壑船与虹桥板已经较少，据多次文物普查得来的数据，目前已探明武夷山还有悬棺遗存18处，20余具，虹桥板百余块。棺内随葬品有人字纹竹席、细棕、龟形木盘和已碳化的丝、棉、大麻、苎麻等织品，以及陶器、青铜器等生活器皿，经测定均为青铜器时代遗物，距今3,000多年。

Third Bend

Look at the boat-shaped coffins at the third bend,

No one knows when they stopped rowing;

The mulberry field becomes a sea,

The illusion is like a lantern in the wind, wallowing in self-pity.

■ Plank Bridge and Jiahe Boat (Boat-Shaped Coffin)

South of the third bend, Xiaozang Peak stands erect. On the cliff on the east side of the peak, several wooden plank bridges are set in the rock wall crisscrossing between the gaps. Two ancient boat-shaped coffins from ancient Yue are on the plank bridges, half inserted in rock gaps, half suspended in the air. There is also a stone cave in the northern half of Xiaozang Peak, called Feixian Platform, with a boat-shaped coffin in it. According to legend, it contains the bones of thirteen immortals, including Ziqian (Emperor Wei). Another nearby small cave is also crisscrossed with plank bridges. Under a rock there is scholar Wu Zhenwen's inscription on the cliff stone "Jiahe Boat".

Mount Wuyi still retains many "mysteries for thousands of years", among which, one of the most famous is the Plank Bridge and Jiahe Boat. In the peaks of Mount Wuyi, a lot of wooden boards are inserted into the rocks, which are called Xianren (Immortal) Bridges or Rainbow Bridges by villagers. The Jiahe boats hanging above the cliffs are also called "immortal boats". They are mainly distributed along the shoreline of Nine-Bend Stream and on the north face of the Wuyi mountains. The boat-shaped coffins are located 30 to 50 meters high on cliffs and precipices. They were either placed in caves or half-inserted, half-suspended in cracks on the cliff face, supported by plank bridges. Due to the aging and natural corrosion, there are only a few remaining now. According to data obtained from a cultural relics survey, there are more than 20 boat-shaped coffins and over 100 pieces of plank bridges in 18 sites. The burial articles in the coffins contain bamboo mats with herringbone pattern, fine palm, turtle-shaped wooden plates, carbonized silk, cotton, hemp, ramie and other fabrics, as well as living utensils such as pottery and bronze ware. They are all artifacts from the Bronze Age, dating back more than 3,000 years.

小藏峰因此也被称为仙船岩、船场岩，它是武夷山中架壑船棺数量最多、分布最集中的场所。这凌空悬架的惊险胜观，自古就引得人们猜测纷纭。究竟是什么样的生活环境和习俗信仰，使当地先民形成此种殡葬习惯？明代学者郑主忠诗曰："峰名小藏藏何物，万仞悬崖架两船。只为风波翻不着，故留人世几千年。"清代著名小说家蒲松龄听闻武夷船棺的传奇，将它编入《聊斋志异》第九卷《武夷》一文中：

"武夷山有削壁千仞，人每于下拾沉香玉块焉。太守闻之，督数百人作云梯，将造顶以觇其异，三年始成。太守登之，将及巅，见大足伸下，一拇指粗于捣衣杵，大声曰：'不下，将堕矣！'大惊，疾下。才至地，则架木朽折，崩坠无遗。"

于是有人说，船棺能保存到现在，还应该感谢蒲松龄，因为他对太守破坏船棺的图谋，用写入奇闻异录的方式进行了大胆的揭露，起到了警诫后人的作用。

Xiaozang Peak is also known as Immortal Boat Rock or Shipyard Rock. It is the place with the largest number of boat-shaped coffins in Mount Wuyi. Since ancient times, the breathtaking view of this valley of hanging coffins has led to much speculation. What kind of living environment, customs and beliefs made local ancestors form such funeral habits? Zheng Zhuzhong, a scholar of the Ming Dynasty, said, "The name of the peak also means 'hide'. What were they hiding on high cliffs with suspended boats? Being protected against disturbance, they have survived for thousands of years." Pu Songling, a famous novelist in the Qing Dynasty, heard the legend of Wuyi's boat-shaped coffins and wrote about it in *Wuyi*, the ninth volume of *Collection of Bizarre Stories*.

"There are thousands of cliffs on Mount Wuyi. People often collected pieces of agarwood and jade from below the cliffs. Then an official appointed hundreds of workers to make aerial ladders. He wanted to learn the secrets of this unique place. However, when he reached the top, he saw an enormous foot stretch out, the big toe of which was like a large pestle and a voice yelled, 'Get out from here quickly, or you will fall to death!' He hurried down to the ground, and then the frame of the wood ladder disintegrated and collapsed completely."

It is said that this is one reason that the boat-shaped coffins have been preserved to the present, and we should thank Pu Songling—as he created the superstitious story to ward off any future plots by officials.

◎ 三曲小藏峰。（郑友裕 摄）
Xiaozang Peak at the third bend. (Photo by Zheng Youyu)

◎ 四曲大藏峰。（郑友裕 摄）

Dazang Peak at the fourth bend. (Photo by Zheng Youyu)

四曲

四曲东西两石岩，

岩花垂露碧㲯㲯；

金鸡叫罢无人见，

月满空山水满潭。

■ 大藏峰

四曲溪水两侧，两座巍巍巨石隔水对峙，成一胜观。东边大藏峰耸拔入云，西边仙钓台临水而立，舟行其间，目之所及均为峭崖峻壁。

大藏峰有"三绝"：巨岩、幽洞与深潭。

先说"一绝"，岩峰巨大，削崖横空，半壁斜覆，行舟于此，顿感"日午吹阴风，昼气黯若夕"。宋陈范有诗道："半岩欲堕潭渚深，昼阳不到午阴阴；洞箫一曲瑶笙断，千山万山云水沉。"

Fourth Bend

There are two rocks to the east and west,

Dew drops on the rock flowers and their green twigs;

No one will see the cock when hearing it crow,

The moon fills the mountain—the water fills the pond.

Dazang Peak

On two sides of the fourth bend, two giant stone rocks stand by the water, creating a wonderful scene. Dazang Peak soars straight into the clouds in the east; Xiandiao (Immortals' Fishing) Platform stands in the west, and along the shoreline, as far as you can see, there are steep cliff walls.

Dazang Peak has three unique features: a giant rock, secluded caves and a deep pool.

The "First Wonder"—a huge rock peak and cliff hanging in the sky, half of the cliff is leaning, so when the bamboo rafts pass here, visitors feel "the afternoon wind blowing on an overcast sky, as dimly as evening". Chen Fan in the Song Dynasty had a poem:

Half of the rock is about to fall,

It's dark even at noon since the sunlight can't fall;

After a song from the bamboo flute, the Sheng (a reed pipe wind instrument) was broken,

And thousands of mountains and clouds sank in the water.

◎ 四曲崖壁上的架壑船遗存。（宋春 摄）
The remains of boat-shaped coffins in the cliff wall at the fourth bend. (Photo by Song Chun)

再说"二绝",从岩下向上望,可见岩峰半壁有一上一下两个洞穴,上为鸡窠岩,相传为古代水鸟的遗巢;下名金鸡洞,洞口虹桥板杂乱堆放,洞内有船棺。洞里还有其他何古物,眼下还是个谜。

"三绝"为大藏峰下的卧龙潭,一泓凝碧深邃莫测,漂游其上,飞翠流霞,云影共天光,人语棹声,互为回应,别有情趣。相传远古年代曾有一恶龙盘踞此潭,时常率九子搅得山崩水啸,天昏地暗,仙人许旌阳路过此地,斩杀九龙,唯一幼龙哀告乞怜,愿改邪归正,于是仙人手下留情,命其潜居潭中,护佑武夷。传说久远不可信,但是每个游客到此或许都会觉得似曾相识,因为在中国家喻户晓的电视剧《西游记》中,小白龙腾出水面的镜头就是在这里拍摄的。

◎ 四曲摩崖石刻。（郑友裕 摄）
The cliff inscription at the fourth bend. (Photo by Zheng Youyu)

The "Second Wonder"—Looking up at the rock from below, you can see that there are two caves in the cliff. The one on top is Jike (Bird Nest) Cave, and according to legend it is the nesting place of ancient waterfowls. The other one below is called Jinji (Golden Chicken) Cave; in front of the cave there are some planks stacked in a disorderly manner, and inside are boat-shaped coffins. What else was in the cave long ago remains a mystery.

The "Third Wonder" is the Wolong (Crouching Dragon) Pool under Dazang Peak. Floating on this deep unfathomable green pool under billowing clouds, people talk and the rowing responds … a lot of fun. Legend has it that in ancient times there was an evil dragon in this pool, whose nine sons tore up the mountain and stirred the water. The sky and the earth became dim, and then the immortal, Xu Jingyang, who passed through here, killed the dragons, except for one young dragon who begged for mercy. The dragon was willing to change his behavior so the immortal showed compassion and said, "Let him live in the pool to protect Wuyi." The legend is from a long time ago and hard to believe, but every Chinese visitor may feel there is something familiar here, because the little white dragon flying out of the water was filmed here in the famous Chinese TV series *Journey to the West*.

◎ 四曲卧龙潭。（郑友裕 摄）

Wolong (Crouching Dragon) Pool at the fourth bend (Photo by Zheng Youyu)

◎ "小九曲"摩崖石刻。（宋春 摄）

"Xiao Jiuqu" (Little Nine-Bend) cliff inscription. (Photo by Song Chun)

　　品玩溪东人间三绝之后，再来赏溪西的仙家钓台。仙钓台岩顶昂首云天，峰影如画，峰腰有真武洞，相传为仙人垂钓之所。移舟换景，待至岩体西壁，又仿佛看到一艘翘首待发的古船，筏工会风趣地告诉游客这是"泰坦尼克"号。

　　四曲不仅有胜观，还有小景，名曰小九曲。小九曲一湾碧水，坻石罗布，溪流萦折，溯洄而入，别有幽复，犹如九曲的小影。现代作家施蛰存曾在诗中这样描写它："偶逢山外山，遂得曲中曲。"相传"小九曲"摩崖石刻是朱熹的真迹。

　　真山水，胜观里投入见细节，小景中忘我生整体，就像照见冬天树林里的每一个因果关系，亲历而后安住。

After enjoying the three wonders on the east shore, come to appreciate the Immortals' Fishing Platform on the west side of the stream. The rock peak soars into the clouds, the shadow of which is very picturesque across the stream and lowlands. On the peak waist there is Zhenwu Cave, which, according to legend, was a place for the immortals to fish. As the boat drifts, the scenery changes, and now you can see that the rock on the west palisades looks like an ancient ship ready for sailing. The rafters joke with visitors, calling it the Titanic.

The fourth bend not only has beautiful scenic views, but also has small curves which people call "Xiao Jiuqu (Little Nine-Bend)". Little Nine-Bend's clear water, with a strand of stones scattered about through which the currents and eddies wind their way, creates a replica of the larger nine bends. Shi Zhecun, a modern writer, once wrote a poem for it: "(You) occasionally meet a mountain outside the mountains, and a bend inside the bends." It is said that "Xiao Jiuqu" cliff inscription is the authentic work of Zhu Xi.

In this surreal landscape, watch the changing scene, immerse yourself in the small sceneries and become the whole, like seeing every cause and effect in the winter forest and then gradually entering the scene.

© 仙钓台。（郑友裕 摄）
The Immortals' Fishing Platform. (Photo by Zheng Youyu)

■ 御茶园

四曲溪南有一片依山傍水的平地，是元代皇家御茶园的故址。御茶园创设于元代，荒废于明代，持续了270多年，见证了武夷茶的兴盛和衰败，是武夷茶史的重要一页。

御茶园曾筑有高台，称为喊山台。每年惊蛰这一天，御茶园官吏偕县丞等带着牲醴，登临喊山台，祭祀茶神，举行喊山仪式，以祈求神灵福佑茶事顺利。古祭文如下：

"惟神，默运化机，地钟和气，物产灵芽，先春特异，石乳流香，龙团佳味，贡于天子，万年无替！资尔神功，用伸常祭。"

念罢祭文，隶卒鸣金击鼓，齐声高喊："茶发芽，茶发芽！"

喊山之后，人们才开山采茶，所以喊山是采茶与制茶之前的一个时间临界点，使人们从平常日子过渡到紧张繁忙的茶季。现在的喊山仪式沿用古祭文，文中的"石乳流香，龙团佳味"是对武夷茶作为贡茶的品质描述，也是传承所在。

■ Royal Tea Plantation

South of the fourth bend, there is a flat stretch of land—the Yuan Dynasty Royal Tea Plantation Site. The royal tea plantation was founded in the Yuan Dynasty and later abandoned in the Ming Dynasty. It lasted for more than 270 years and witnessed the rise and fall of Wuyi Tea, which was an important period in the history of tea at Mount Wuyi.

There used to be a high platform at the Royal Tea Plantation, known as Hanshan (Mountain Shouting) Platform. On the day of the Waking of Insects (3rd solar term) every year, officials came to the mountain to offer sacrifice to the tea gods. The "Mountain Shouting Ceremony" was held at that time to pray for gods' blessings for the tea. The ancient song goes as follows:

"Tea gods, gather the energy from the sky and earth to produce the fresh new bud in the first days of spring; the stone milk (water in rocks) flows with fragrance to breed the dragon ball (tea) which tastes fine; we will give it to the son of heaven as a tribute which can't be replaced forever! Thanks for the miraculous power from the gods; let the sacrifice be held often."

After the ceremony, the villagers start to drum and shout: "Tea germinate; tea germinate!"

After the shouting, people start to pick the topmost tea leaves, so "Mountain Shouting" is a critical time before tea picking and making, transitioning the villagers from their normal days to the busy tea season. The present mountain shouting ceremony still follows the ancient ritual, and "The stone milk flows with fragrance to breed the dragon ball (tea) which tastes fine." is a description of Wuyi tea's quality as tribute tea, and its cultural inheritance.

◎ 四季御茶园。（郑友裕 摄）
The Royal Tea Plantation in four seasons. (Photo by Zheng Youyu)

◎ 隐屏峰。（郑友裕 摄）
Yinping Peak. (Photo by Zheng Youyu)

五曲

五曲山高云气深，

长时烟雨暗平林；

林间有客无人识，

欸乃声中万古心。

■ 武夷精舍

　　五曲溪畔隐屏峰下的平林渡有武夷精舍故址。武夷精舍又名武夷书院、紫阳书院，由朱熹于宋淳熙十年（1183）亲自擘画、营建，布局精妙，营建艰苦：

　　"……而于其溪之五折，负大石屏，规之以为精舍，取道士之庐犹半也。诛锄茅草，仅得数亩。面势幽清，奇石佳林，拱揖映带，若阴相而遗我者。使弟子辈具畚锸、集瓦木，相率成之。元晦躬画其处，中以为堂，旁以为斋，高以为亭，密以为室，讲书肄业，琴歌酒赋，莫不在是。"

　　精舍落成，"四方士友来者亦甚众，莫不叹其佳胜"。朱熹赋诗《精舍杂咏十二首》以作纪念，并邀请了建宁知府、著名词人韩元吉和史学家袁枢等密友前来庆贺。韩元吉作《武夷精舍记》，不仅记下了上文所引的建造过程，还借"舞雩之风"的典故，赞其"幔亭之风"；袁枢贺诗"此志未可量，见之千载后"；诗人陆游也驰函寄贺诗四首。

Fifth Bend

The mountains at the fifth bend are high and the clouds are thick,

Eternal misty rains dampen the forest;

Among the trees no one knows who the guests are,

The heart goes on forever, sculling in the creek.

■ Wuyi Academy

Wuyi Academy Site is located at Pinglin Ferry at the foot of Yinping Peak by the fifth bend. Wuyi Academy, also known as Ziyang Academy, was personally designed and built by Zhu Xi in 1183, with an exquisite layout and sturdy construction:

"… At the fifth bend, he put a big stone to signify the place to build a nice leisure cottage on a few acres. It is quiet and serene, and with unique stones and beautiful trees. Yuan Hui (Zhu Xi) made his disciples prepare the ground, collect the tiles and wood and start to build. He painted all the rooms by himself, including the middle hall, the side study rooms, the high pavilion, and some other rooms where they could teach, play instruments, sing, and write poetry."

After the completion of the cottage Zhu Xi wrote, "Many friends came from everywhere, and all admired this wonderful place." He wrote 12 poems about this special place to commemorate it, and invited the governor of Jianning, the famous poet Han Yuanji, the historian Yuan Shu and other close friends to celebrate with him. Han Yuanji wrote *A Memorandum of Wuyi Academy*, not only noting the construction process cited above, but also made an allusion to the "Spirit of Wuyu", praising its "Spirit of Manting". Yuan Shu wrote in his poem, "This ambitious undertaking cannot be measured; you will only realize (its significance) after a thousand years." The famous Song Dynasty poet Lu You also sent letters with four poems as congratulations.

◎ 武夷精舍故址。（郑友裕 摄）
Wuyi Academy Site.
(Photo by Zheng Youyu)

◎ 精舍讲堂。（郑友裕 摄）
The lecture room. (Photo by Zheng Youyu)

　　武夷精舍门前有茶灶石，朱熹以《茶灶》一诗记之："仙翁遗石灶，宛在水中央。饮罢方舟去，茶烟袅细香。"在武夷精舍，朱熹与门人士友们诗意栖居，挟书而诵，无疑是自由快乐的。他在给好友陈亮的信中说："武夷九曲之中，比缚得小屋三数间，可以游息，春间尝一到，留止旬余。溪山回合，云烟开敛，旦暮万状，信非人境也。"

　　朱熹在武夷精舍广收门徒，倡道讲学，著书立说。书院开办期间，理学学术活动活跃，朱熹的思想体系也逐步走向成熟，陆续完成十余部著作，其中包括他的重要代表作《四书集注》。当时，许多名噪东南的学者，如蔡元定、游九言、李方子、黄干等人纷至沓来，受业于朱熹门下，书院因此被现代海内外学者喻为"中国第一所私立大学"。

　　书院传播布道形式灵活，内容具实，从修身、齐家到举止礼仪、改正错误等，与日常融合，有着强大的号召力。借助建本技术，朱熹将自己和同仁的著作刊发天下；数百名学者、弟子走出这所书院，载道前往四面八方，推动了儒学新的复兴，为重新树立起儒家思想的正宗地位奠定了牢固的基石。

here is a tea-stove stone in front of Wuyi Academy, about which Zhu Xi wrote in a poem called *Tea-Stove*:

Immortals placed the stone stove here;
It looks like it's in the middle of the water.
After drinking, the boat is gone;
There's a fine fragrance lingering in the air.

hu Xi and his friends enjoyed living here writing poetry, reading books, discoursing about their thoughts … It must have been a carefree, happy time. a letter to his friend Chen Liang, he said, "Among the ne bends of Wuyi, I have several small houses where can stroll about and rest for a few days when spring omes. The stream goes around the mountains, clouds pating in the sky, and it all changes from morning to ghtfall … Heaven!"

hu Xi gathered disciples here, taught and wrote ooks. Ever since the opening of Wuyi Academy, he academic activities of Neo-Confucianism were ctive here, and Zhu Xi's ideological system gradually natured. He successively completed more than ten orks, including his important seminal work *Variorum r the Four Books*. At that time, many famous scholars southeast China, such as Cai Yuanding, You Jiuyan, Li angzi, Huang Gan, etc., came here in great numbers

◎ 茶灶石。（郑友裕 摄）
Tea-stove stone. (Photo by Zheng Youyu)

nd were taught by Zhu Xi. Today, the academy is called "the first private university in China" by modern scholars home and abroad.

he academy's curriculum was flexible in form and substantial in content, from cultivating one's morality and eeping one's filial duties to practicing etiquette and correcting mistakes, etc., all integrating with experiences from ne's daily life. It had a strong appeal at the time throughout China. With the help of the exquisite block printing echnology in Jianyang, Zhu Xi and his colleagues cooperated to publish the works and spread his teaching all over he country. Hundreds of scholars and disciples went out from the academy travelling in all directions, promoting a ew revival of Confucianism and laying a solid foundation for re-establishing the premier position of Confucianism Chinese thought.

孔子以"智者乐水，仁者乐山"比德山水，朱熹则自号武夷精舍的"仁智堂主"，他在《武夷精舍杂咏并序·仁智堂》中写道："吾惭仁智心，偶自爱山水。"仁智者，总能通过观想自然山水建立起自己的世界观。正如约翰·海恩斯在《星星、雪、火》里所写的："我所开辟的路，通往外在的山坡和沼泽，也通往心中的丘壑。"古时书院于山水自然间和乐自由地悦志悦神，于思辩结合、教学相长的氛围中专注学问，所倡导的"修身、处事、接物"的书院文化精神，现今可转化为"自由灵动、崇尚思考、立德立人"的亲历游学来践履。

五曲溪流两旁丹崖林立，隐屏峰峭拔，左倚玉华峰，右依接笋峰，耸峙于平林渡。溪南岸依次有更衣台、天柱峰和晚对峰；西岸有仙迹岩和太姥岩。行舟至此，苍石翠屏，石峰簇秀，左顾右盼，应接不暇。

Confucius once said, "The wise man takes pleasure in waters, the benevolent man takes pleasure in the mountains." At Wuyi Academy Zhu Xi called himself the "master of the wise and benevolent". A wise man can always establish his own world view by looking at the natural landscape. As John Haines wrote in *The Stars, the Snow, the Fire*: "The path I have made leads to the hills and marshes, and to the gully within." In those ancient times, the academies situated in the beautiful natural setting of these mountains not only nurtured the ambition and spirit freely, but also focused on seeking knowledge in an atmosphere of learning and teaching. Their cultural essence of "cultivating one's morality, by doing things, and receiving things" is read today as "free and etheric, advocating learning and thinking, building people's moral integrity through practice".

There are red cliffs bristling on both sides of the stream at the fifth bend. Yinping Peak is steep and straight with Yuhua Peak on the left and Jiesun Peak on the right, rising over Pinglin Ferry. On the south bank of the stream, there are Gengyi (Dressing) Platform, Tianzhu Peak and Wandui Peak. There is also Xianji (Fairy Trace) Rock and Taimu Rock on the west bank. Coming in a boat here, and viewing the huge rocks and jade green peaks making a cluster galaxy … you will be overwhelmed as you look left or right.

© 更衣台。（郑友裕 摄）
The Dressing Platform. (Photo by Zheng Youyu)

◎ 茶洞。（黄恒日 摄）

Tea Canyon. (Photo by Huang Hengri)

■ 茶洞

接笋峰下，从伏虎岩东行，穿过巨石垒叠的石门，至一幽深处，即"茶洞"。据史料记载，昔日茶洞一带所产之茶，有"甲于武夷"之说。清李卷曾题诗赞其茶："乳花香泛清虚味，旗枪浮绿压醒醐。"

徐霞客描述茶洞："诸峰上皆峭绝，而下复攒凑，外无磴道，独西通一罅，比天台之明岩更为奇矫也。"由此可知茶洞之奇，更是因为它"峥嵘深锁"的境界。这一岩间谷地，四周攒立了七座巍巍峰岩——接笋峰、隐屏峰、玉华峰、天游峰、清隐岩、仙掌峰和仙游岩，诸峰环护，只有西边有一通路。人于其间，就像隐陷井底，抬望只能窥见青天一围。

茶洞有留云书屋、望仙楼遗址，立此尽收溪山之致，董天工的《武夷山志》就是在望仙楼汇编完成的。说来有趣，历代有不少人在这里卜筑隐居，唐代僧人建石堂寺，宋代刘衡建小隐堂，明代李钟鼎建煮霞居，清代潘银台建武夷别业、董茂勋建留云书屋和晚霞居、董天工建望仙楼，可见这里自古就是幽深绝尘之处。

■ Tea Canyon

Start from Crouching Tiger Rock to the east under Jiesun Peak, go through a stone gate stacked with huge boulders, and you can get to a hidden place called "Tea Canyon". According to historical records, the tea produced here was the best tea in Mount Wuyi. Li Juan in the Qing Dynasty once wrote a poem praising this tea: "Fragrance of milk and flowers drifts the aroma; floating leaves will keep your mind clear."

Xu Xiake describes Tea Canyon like this: "All the mountains around are steep; there is no way inside except a crack on the west; it is more unique than the Ming Rock on Mount Tiantai." Tea Canyon is unique because it is like an "extraordinarily deep loch" surrounded by seven lofty peaks and steep rocks—Jiesun Peak, Yinping Peak, Yuhua Peak, Tianyou (Heavenly Tour) Peak, Qingyin Rock, Xianzhang Peak and Xianyou Rock, with only one access path in from the west. A man in here is like in the bottom of a well, who can only see a piece of the blue sky when he looks up.

At Tea Canyon there are the ruins of Liuyun Study and Wangxian Tower, which makes for a perfect scene with the stream and mountains. Dong Tiangong's *Records of Mount Wuyi* was compiled in Wangxian Tower. Many people from past dynasties came here for seclusion and to build places of reflection and study: A monk in the Tang Dynasty built Shitang Temple; Liu Heng in the Song Dynasty built Xiaoyin Hall; Li Zhongding in the Ming Dynasty built the Zhuxia House; in the Qing Dynasty Pan Yintai built Wuyi Villa, Dong Maoxun built Liuyun Library and Wanxia House, and Dong Tiangong built Wangxian Tower. From ancient times and dynasties, Tea Canyon has been a special place for pondering and discussing the mysteries of the universe.

◎ 茶洞碑文。（宋春 摄）

The tablet inscription at Tea Canyon. (Photo by Song Chun)

■ 竞台

从平林渡去往茶洞，途经一方摩崖石刻，上书"竞台"二字。下面有一石台，台面平整，被称为"评茶台"，这便是宋代建州斗茶之处了。聚集于竞台之下，于评茶台上摆开斗茶的茶品，参与者轮流品尝，以决高下，斗胜者的茶品立即红绫披覆，黄缎加裹，成为"官茶"。

斗茶又叫"茗战"，源于唐代，兴于宋代。北宋初年，朝野上下饮茶风尚盛极一时，茶争奇，器斗妍。宋代著名文学家范仲淹所作《和章岷从事斗茶歌》中有一句"黄金碾畔绿尘飞，碧玉瓯中翠涛起"，"瓯"指的就是一种喝茶器具——茶盏。

位于武夷山国家级风景名胜区西北部的遇林亭窑址，是武夷山被联合国教科文组织列入世界文化与自然遗产名录的重要内容之一。这一宋代的瓷窑遗址出土了大量宋代黑釉、青釉瓷器及窑具标本，以茶盏类最为大宗，其中一批"描金、银彩"的黑釉瓷碗，在中国同类窑址中属首次发现，在国际传世品种中极为罕见。

探访拥有两座龙窑的遇林亭遗址，听一听风雨亭的故事，回程时在武夷山知名的永生泉打一桶甘洌清甜的山泉水，泡一壶武夷岩茶，你也可以细细揣摩茶与茶具的相互成就。

■ Jing Tai (Competition Platform)

Along the way from the Pinglin Ferry to Tea Canyon, there is a cliff stone inscription—just two words "Jing Tai". Below it there is a flat stone table, known as the "Tea Table", and this is where during the Song Dynasty people had the tea competitions. Villagers gathered under the cliff and set out the tea competition utensils on this tea evaluation platform. Judges took turns tasting the tea to decide the superior ones. The winning tea was immediately covered with red silk and wrapped with yellow satin to become the "official tea".

Tea competitions, also known as "tea wars", actually originated during the Tang Dynasty but flourished in the Song Dynasty. In the early years of the Northern Song Dynasty, the fashion of drinking tea was extremely popular. Fan Zhongyan, a famous literary author in the Song Dynasty, wrote a poem to describe the tea competition with his friend Zhang Min, and there is a line which tells of "Green dust flies in the golden pan, and green waves swirl in the jade cups." The "cups" here are very special local tea cups.

Yulin Pavilion Kiln Site in the northwest of Wuyishan National Scenic Area is one of the most important sites in Mount Wuyi inscribed on the World Heritage list. At this archaeological kiln site they have unearthed a large number of Song Dynasty black glaze and blue glaze porcelains and also kiln manufacturing artifacts. The tea cup styles were varied, among which a group of "painted gold and silver color" on black glaze porcelain bowls were found for the first time in China—something very rare even among the surviving varieties internationally.

Come visit the two dragon kilns at Yulin Pavilion Site, listen to the story of Fengyu (Wind and Rain) Pavilion, and when you return, go to Mount Wuyi's famous Eternal Stream to get a bucket of sweet mountain spring water and brew a pot of Wuyi Rock Tea. This is the best way to really feel the relationship between the mountains, streams, tea, and tea sets during the Mount Wuyi tea ceremony. And later, wherever you may be, when you enjoy Wuyi Rock Tea, you will remember that special feeling again.

◎ 遇林亭窑址。（郑友裕 摄）
Yulin Pavilion Kiln Site. (Photo by Zheng Youyu)

和章岷从事斗茶歌

[宋]范仲淹

年年春自东南来，建溪先暖冰微开。

溪边奇茗冠天下，武夷仙人从古栽。

新雷昨夜发何处，家家嬉笑穿云去。

露芽错落一番荣，缀玉含珠散嘉树。

终朝采掇未盈襜，唯求精粹不敢贪。

研膏焙乳有雅制，方中圭兮圆中蟾。

北苑将期献天子，林下雄豪先斗美。

鼎磨云外首山铜，瓶携江上中泠水。

黄金碾畔绿尘飞，碧玉瓯中翠涛起。

斗茶味兮轻醍醐，斗茶香兮薄兰芷。

其间品第胡能欺，十目视而十手指。

胜若登仙不可攀，输同降将无穷耻。

吁嗟天产石上英，论功不愧阶前蓂。

众人之浊我可清，千日之醉我可醒。

屈原试与招魂魄，刘伶却得闻雷霆。

卢仝敢不歌，陆羽须作经。

森然万象中，焉知无茶星。

商山丈人休茹芝，首阳先生休采薇。

长安酒价减千万，成都药市无光辉。

不如仙山一啜好，泠然便欲乘风飞。

君莫羡，花间女郎只斗草，赢得珠玑满斗归。

　　《和章岷从事斗茶歌》除了写到奇茗、美器之外，还涉及茶的品鉴、茶艺的切磋，以及采茶、焙茶、制茶等内容，脍炙人口。

　　武夷茶事的兴盛也反映在五曲岩壁的摩崖石刻上，有"庞公吃茶处""应接不暇"等勒刻于丹岩之上。其中保护武夷茶生产者利益的檄文《严禁买茶短价告示》的摩崖石刻尤其值得一提，告示声明严禁买茶短价等各种劣行，对于违反者"照律治罪""决不宽容"。

　　这些胜地与胜迹，这些茶与茶事，仿佛在默默诉说着：他们曾经这样活过。

A popular poem from Fan Zhongyan not only talks about the superb tea and beautiful vessels, but also evokes the essence of tea tasting, the art of tea, as well as tea picking, tea baking, tea making and other unique aspects of tea.

The popularity of Wuyi tea is also reflected in the cliff inscriptions at the fifth bend, e.g. the inscriptions of "Where Panggong (a recluse obsessed with tea) drank tea" and "Too many (beautiful scenes) to see" are carved on the red cliffs. Also among them, you'll see the official regulations to protect the interests of tea producers in Wuyi called "Notice Against Buying Tea at a Low Price", which are particularly worth mentioning. The notice states that it is strictly forbidden to buy tea at a low price or do other bad behavior, or the violators will be "punished according to law" with "no toleration". These regulations were designed to maintain a good price for the tea so the farmers could make a living.

These resorts, along with the tea and tea events … silently whisper, "They once lived this way."

◎ 五曲摩崖石刻。（郑友裕 摄）

The cliff inscriptions at the fifth bend. (Photo by Zheng Youyu)

◎ 斗茶赛现场。（郑友裕 摄）
The scene of a tea competition. (Photo by Zheng Youyu)

宋代斗茶作为评定茶叶品质高下的特殊活动，起初在贵族间流行，后在民间普及，其中斗胜茶品也会被纳入贡茶。如今贡茶早已成为历史，斗茶之风却得以在武夷山地区保留。武夷山每年11月都会举办盛大的茶博会，如同当地茶业界的嘉年华，各种民间斗茶活动也大多在这期间举行。斗茶赛上既能喝一回价值不菲的百家茶，又能结识各种高人，现场通常人山人海，连英国BBC电台都曾专程前来拍摄。如果你能亲临现场，不但可以体验千姿百态的茶趣，还可以报名成为大众评委，参与品评。对于一些入门级的茶友来说，斗茶赛仿佛一场大考，而他们便如参加考试的学生，急着和业界大神对答案，看看自己猜中了几分。

决赛环节会筛选出四五十种茶样，每一茶样依照审评标准程序，接受三轮的品评，由大众评委和专家评委从色、香、味、形等方面按照一定的权重打分。要想不喝晕，那是要有真功夫呢！

斗茶，把匠人的境界、品味、技艺从规定动作中体现出来，荣获状元的茶品正可谓"斗茶味分轻醍醐，斗茶香分薄兰芷"，展现着有如贡茶的优秀品质，业界泰斗、民间高手也可以于此间与古为徒，体会传承。

In the Song Dynasty the tea competition was a special activity to assess the quality of tea, initially prevalent among the nobles, and then popular with the village folk, in which the winning tea may become the tribute tea. Paying tea as a tribute was a thing of the past; however, the spirit of tea competition has been preserved in Mount Wuyi. Every November Wuyishan holds a grand tea fair, like a tea exposition, and a variety of local tea competition activities are also held during this period. During the tea competition, you can drink many valuable teas, and get to meet a variety of tea experts. The famous competition hosts a sea of people from around the world; even one year, the British BBC TV filmed the event. If you visit this event, you can experience some enjoyable tea activities, and even sign up to become a tea judge and participate in the evaluation. For some novice tea lovers, the tea competition is like a big test, and they are like students taking the exam, anxious to see their selection win the most points.

The final winner will be selected from over forty to fifty different kinds of tea samples; each tea sample is measured by standard procedures, with three rounds of evaluation by the public judges and expert judges for color, aroma, taste, shape and other aspects according to a certain weighted score. If you can drink all the teas without tea-drunkenness, you have real kung fu!

The competition affords different teas an opportunity to show tea-makers' realm, taste and techniques. The winning one is said to "enlighten the tongue like wine with a scent like vanilla", which displays an excellent quality like the Song Dynasty tribute tea. In the meantime, connoisseurs and folk masters imitate ancient ways and make themselves part of the heritage.

◎ 茶样。（宋春 摄）

Tea samples. (Photo by Song Chun)

◎ 位于天游峰峰顶的天游观。（郑友裕 摄）
Tianyou Monastery at Tianyou Peak. (Photo by Zheng Youyu)

六曲

六曲苍屏绕碧湾，

茅茨终日掩柴关；

客来倚棹岩花落，

猿鸟不惊春意闲。

■ 天游峰

六曲有被徐霞客赞为"武夷第一胜地"的天游峰。要赏九曲山水全景，再也找不到比天游峰更好的地方。

Sixth Bend

Verdant screen encircles the green bay,

Thatched houses always close their wood doors;

Visitors leaning on the oars, the flowers on the rocks fall,

Apes and birds are not afraid of humans during the springtime.

Tianyou (Heavenly Tour) Peak

Tianyou Peak at the sixth bend has been praised by Xu Xiake as "Wuyi's First Resort". And there is no better place than Tianyou Peak to enjoy the panoramic view of the mountains and the stream of nine bends.

◎ 洞中望天游。（郑友裕 摄）
Tianyou Peak seen from the cave. (Photo by Zheng Youyu)

天游峰壁立万仞，高耸于群峰之上，自成一体，登临其巅，纵览群峰，俯瞰九曲，溪山全态一览而尽，正是："山耸千层青翡翠，溪流九曲碧琉璃。"每当雨后乍晴、晨曦初露之时，白茫茫的云雾弥山漫谷，变幻莫测。此时若能登峰巅，望云海，便宛如置身于蓬莱仙境，遨游于天宫琼阁，"天游"两字，实至名归。

　　天游峰有上、下之分，一览亭左，是为上天游；下有崎岖丘，沿胡麻涧一带，是为下天游。

　　上天游的一览亭濒临悬崖，高踞万仞之巅，是一座绝好的观赏台。明代诗人钱秉镫诗赞："闻到天游客罢游，果然此踞最高头。方知曲曲山回转，合使峰峰水抱流。丹碧皴中通估舶，烟云破处垦田畴。棹歌不向前途去，一览台边已尽收。"

◎ "十六洞天"摩崖石刻。（宋春 摄）
The cliff inscription "Sixteen caves". (Photo by Song Chun)

　　下天游胡麻涧由山南蜿蜒而来，自妙高台西面奔泻而下，形成了著名的雪花泉景观。涧之两侧的峭崖之上有历代摩崖石刻三十余处，连绵约百米，有"仙凡混合""福地洞天""十六洞天""无量寿佛""寿""第一山""武夷第一峰""竞秀争妍""奇胜天台"等等。

　　六曲有"岩壁第一"的仙掌峰，这个定评来自明代汪桂《武夷山游记》里的评述："仙掌一峰，堵天障海，铁肤冰棱，如万丈翠涛，天风吹立，宜为岩壁第一。"仙掌峰长年被水冲刷，石面上布满了直直的流水轨迹，赶上雨天，水便从峰顶顺着这些轨迹飞泻直下，映着天光闪闪发亮，就像素练披在山崖上，妙不可言，堪称奇景。所以它又有一个别名，叫作晒布岩。

© 天游峰顶俯瞰九曲。（郑友裕 摄）
Overlooking Nine-Bend Stream from Tianyou Peak. (Photo by Zheng Youyu)

Tianyou Peak towers over a group of other peaks. You can climb to the top and scan all the peaks overlooking the nine bends. When the sun comes out after a rain, or in the early morning dew, the white clouds spread over the valley, in an undulating purifying blanket. At this time, if you can stand on the peak, and look out over the sea of clouds, it is like being in heaven, "Tianyou (Heavenly Tour)"—two well deserved words.

Tianyou Peak has two parts—The left side of Yilan Pavilion is called "Rising Tianyou"; and along the Huma Stream area there are rugged hills, which are called "Descending Tianyou".

The Yilan Pavilion along Rising Tianyou is on the edge of a cliff, perched high on the top of a hundred peaks, and provides an excellent panoramic view. Ming Dynasty poet Qian Bingdeng even wrote a poem to praise this place.

Huma Stream in the Descending Tianyou winds down from the south side of the mountain to form the famous Xuehua (Snow) Spring landscape down the west side of Miaogao Platform. On the cliffs on both sides of the stream, there are over 30 cliff inscriptions from past dynasties, stretching for about 100 meters. You will see "Celestials and mortals mixing", "A blessed spot", "Sixteen caves", "Boundless longevity Buddha", "Longevity", "The first mountain", "The first peak of Wuyi", "Beauty competition", "Spectacular heaven platform", etc.

There is also Xianzhang Peak, known as "The first rock wall", at the sixth bend, which is affirmed in *The Travel Notes to Mount Wuyi* written by Wang Gui in the Ming Dynasty: "Xianzhang Peak, rising into the sky, like a hundred-meter-high green wave, with the wind blowing, is the most imposing rock wall." Xianzhang Peak was scoured by water for many centuries, carving straight vertical tracks down the stone. On rainy days, water from the top of these tracks flies straight down, reflecting the shining sunlight, which looks like white silk ribbons flowing down the cliff. This is why it also has another name, Shaibu (Cloth Drying) Rock. What a wonderful sight!

© 晒布岩。（郑友裕 摄）
Shaibu (Cloth Drying) Rock. (Photo by Zheng Youyu)

◎ 桃源洞道观。（郑友裕 摄）
The Taoist temple at Taoyuan Cave. (Photo by Zheng Youyu)

■ 桃源洞

　　六曲有桃源洞，藏于深山之中，因为"风光近武陵"，又得"小桃源"之名。徐霞客在《游武夷山日记》中赞曰："有地一区，四山环绕，中有平畴曲涧，围以苍松翠竹，鸡声人语，俱在翠微中。"

　　若从天游景区沿着松鼠涧北行，去往桃源洞，一路更能得陶渊明《桃花源记》的真况味。涧溪沿着山径曲折萦洄，岩壁上不时有题刻现于眼前，"疑无路""问津处""仙源"……虚虚实实，颇多乐趣。行至一由岩石崩塌堆积而成的岩洞处，俯身小心地迂回而过，洞口便可见小桃源石门。门楣额书"桃源洞"，两侧有一对楹联："喜无樵子复观奕（弈），怕有渔郎来问津。"穿过石门，眼前豁然开朗，青山四合中有一平旷之地，建有道观。春季来此，但见桃花灼灼。

▨ Taoyuan (Peach Blossom) Cave

Taoyuan Cave is located near the sixth bend, which is hidden between the mountains and the scenery is like that of a paradise. Xu Xiake said in his *Diaries of the Trip to Mount Wuyi*: "There is a land area with mountains on each side, in which there is a flat field and crooked stream, surrounded by green pines and bamboo, with the sound of chickens and humans, all around the green."

If you travel north along Songshu (Squirrel) Stream from Tianyou Scenic Area to Taoyuan Cave, you can get the true flavor of Tao Yuanming's (a very famous Chinese poet in the Eastern Jin Dynasty) work *A Journey to the Land of Peach Blossoms*. The stream twists and turns along the mountain path; the inscriptions on the rock walls, "Doubt no road", "A place to ask", "Fairy source", make you wonder what these ancient scribes were thinking. Go to the place where the rock wall has collapsed creating a cave … bend over carefully and you can see a small stone gate at the entrance. "Taoyuan Cave" was written on the lintel over the gate, flanked by a pair of poetic couplets. Your eyes suddenly light up when you pass through the stone gate—There is a flat piece of land, where Taoyuan Cave Taoist Temple was built many years ago. When you come here in the spring, you can see and smell the peach blossoms.

◎ 小桃源石门。（郑友裕 摄）
The entrance to Taoyuan Cave. (Photo by Zheng Youyu)

◎ 桃源洞老君像。（宋春 摄）
The statue of Lao Tzu at Taoyuan Cave. (Photo by Song Chun)

　　桃源洞有老君像，高16米，宽11米，厚10米，与此天
然环境相映成趣。

　　若遇端午节，午后九曲溪停排，洗河祈福。先观龙
舟，然后漫步到桃源洞，正好赶上午课的诵经声，与蝉鸣
此起彼伏，浑然天成。安坐于小桃源，脑海中回响起《桃
花源记》中那句"不知有汉，无论魏晋"，也会生出不知
身处何时何地之感。

There is a statue of Lao Tzu at Taoyuan Cave, 16 meters high, 11 meters wide and 10 meters thick.

When time comes for the Dragon Boat Festival, the rafts stop in a line in the afternoon on Nine-Bend Stream; the villagers wash the river for a blessing. Travelers can watch the dragon boats first, and then stroll to Taoyuan Cave to listen to the priests chanting following the rhythm of the cicadas chirping one after another, like nature singing in reply. Sitting in there, think about the sentence in *A Journey to the Land of Peach Blossoms*: "I do not know the Han Dynasty, regardless of the Wei and Jin dynasties." You may have a feeling of not knowing where you are yourself or even when it is.

◎ 桃源洞寿桃石。（郑友裕 摄）
A peach-shaped stone with the inscription of "Longevity" at Taoyuan Cave. (Photo by Zheng Youyu)

■ 响声岩

响声岩在六曲溪南临水而立，与东侧的山峰相对，形成一个喇叭形的穹谷，穹谷对面的北岸群峰环峙，于是声音可以在穹谷和北岸峰壁之间往返回荡，久久不息，响声岩的名字便是由此而来。

此处不仅有隐居武夷的明代兵部侍郎陈省所题的"空谷传声"，还镌刻着南宋至清代的23处摩崖石刻，是武夷山摩崖石刻的精华所在。其中朱熹题刻的"逝者如斯"最为引人注目。石刻群中还有朱熹的《九曲棹歌·六曲》及朱熹偕友遨游至此的两方纪游题刻。其中一方刻于淳熙二年（1175），全文为："何叔京、朱仲晦、连嵩卿、蔡季通、徐文臣、吕伯共、潘叔昌、范伯崇、张元善，淳熙乙未五月廿一日。"这幅石刻与中外哲学史上著名的史诗级论辩"鹅湖之会"紧密相连，此为出发前往鹅湖之前，朱熹偕同学友、门生一起游览武夷山，勒石以纪胜。

此外，岩壁上还有宋儒蔡抗、邹应龙和明儒湛若水的纪游题刻，记载了宋明理学在武夷山传播的盛况，亦是武夷山成为"道南理窟"的见证。

"空谷传声，虚堂习听"出自中国古代的蒙学课本《千字文》，简单解释就是，空旷的山谷中呼喊声传得很远，宽敞的厅堂里一处发声各处都会响应。《千字文》里这句之前的两句是："景行维贤，克念作圣。德建名立，形端表正。"德行正大光明，才能成为贤人；克服自己的妄念，才能成为圣人。德行建立起来了，声名自然会树立；心行举止端庄了，仪表自然就会端正。

想来，这才是摩崖石刻得以流传的更深层内涵所在。

■ Xiangsheng (Thundering) Rock

South of the sixth bend, a rock forms a deep, horn-shaped valley with mountains in the east, and peaks along the north bank, so the sounds echo back and forth between the mountains and peak walls for a long time. This is how the rock got the name "Xiangsheng (Thundering) Rock".

Although set in a secluded spot in Wuyi mountains, this rock was inscribed with "An empty valley spreads the voice far away" by Chen Sheng, a minister in the Ming Dynasty, and also carved with 23 additional stone inscriptions from the Southern Song Dynasty to the Qing Dynasty, covering the essence of Mount Wuyi stone inscriptions. Among them Zhu Xi's inscription "Time flies like the water" is the most eye-catching … especially if you just look at the stream for a time. There is also the sixth part of *Nine-Bend Rowing Song* and another two inscriptions of Zhu Xi when he traveled here with his friends. One of them listed Zhu Zhonghui (Zhu Xi's alias) and eight names of his friends in 1175. This stone inscription is closely connected with the world-famous epic debate in the history of Chinese philosophy called "Goose Lake Debate". Before leaving for Goose Lake, Zhu Xi visited Mount Wuyi's Nine-Bend Stream together with his friends and students. (More about the Goose Lake Debate later.)

© 鸣声岩。（郑友裕 摄）
Xiangsheng (Thundering) Rock (Photo by Zheng Youyu)

◎ 鹅湖书院。（阮雪清 摄）
Goose Lake Academy. (Photo by Ruan Xueqing)

In addition, there are inscriptions on the cliff by scholars Cai Kang and Zou Yinglong from the Song Dynasty. Scholar Zhan Ruoshui from the Ming Dynasty, wrote about the great influence of Song and Ming Neo-Confucianism at Mount Wuyi, which is also a witness that Mount Wuyi had become the "grotto of Confucianism in the south".

"An empty valley spreads the voice far away; a sound in the spacious hall will echo everywhere." These two sentences are from the ancient Chinese elementary education textbook *Thousand-Character Classic*. Another two sentences before are:

"He who tries to be virtuous and upright becomes a sage; he who overcomes his own delusion becomes a saint. When virtue is established, fame is naturally established; when the mind is dignified, the appearance will be well-featured."

In a way, the ancient and eternal wisdom behind these words is the reason why the stone inscriptions hold sway even today.

From the translator: Now let's talk about Goose Lake Debate for a minute. As with any great philosophical movement like Zhu Xi's, there were other scholars with different opinions.

Of all the scholars that may have disagreed with Zhu Xi, probably Lu Jiuyuan was the most famous and popular. Lu and his brother met with Zhu Xi at Goose Lake and exchanged viewpoints and later followed up with many letters (some heated). As their disagreement became more pronounced, scholars referred to their disagreement as the "Goose Lake Debate".

Their differences centered on the methodology of becoming a sage—much like what occurred during the split in China Buddhism (Northern School vs Southern School).

Zhu Xi (like Confucius and the Great Vehicle of Buddhism) advocated extensive study and learning of things (ancient texts, life experiences, etc.) in order to find the inner Truth—Zhu Xi spoke of *gradually* understanding the Truth.

Lu Jiuyuan and his brother Lu Jiuling (and later popularized by Wang Yangming) argued that one should focus inward to seek the ultimate Truth in one's own mind and heart (heart/mind). Lu Jiuyuan said, "The universe is my mind; my mind is the universe." It is similar to Buddhist/Hindu/Vedanta philosophies ("Mind is Buddha, Buddha is mind.") and Hui Neng's Southern School concept of instant enlightenment from seeking within ... the heart/mind. Essentially Lu Jiuyuan is saying that it (Truth) is always there inside you—you just need to become aware (awaken to this Truth).

In any event, Zhu Xi's philosophies became the cornerstone of Chinese academia and life for hundreds of years, even though Wang Yangming's "heart/mind" became very popular during the Ming Dynasty.

七曲

七曲移船上碧滩，

隐屏仙掌更回看；

却怜昨夜峰头雨，

添得飞泉几道寒。

▓ 三仰峰

　　武夷山国家级风景名胜区内的最高峰——三仰峰，矗立在七曲溪北。三峰相叠，最高的是大仰，中间的是中仰，最下的是小仰，峰头都朝向东面。登峰四望，武夷山岩如群狮雄踞，如万马奔腾，连绵起伏，一览而收。虽然三仰峰的海拔只有700多米，但是无论是在山南或者山北，抑或在九曲的溪口或溪尾，都可以看到它三峰叠起的巍巍雄姿。清倪天翰赋诗赞三仰峰：

峰连三叠插空斜，

白日寒生翠影遮；

石径多经新玉斧，

井泉尚涌旧丹砂；

沉沉铺绿云中树，

片片流红洞口霞；

至此幽深无俗物，

春风常笑碧桃花。

　　"井泉尚涌旧丹砂""片片流红洞口霞"描述的是三仰峰的小仰。小仰峰半腰有碧霄洞，洞上方岩壁勒有明万历年间林培所书的"武夷最高处"五字。洞旁有一口井，相传为白玉蟾的丹井。据记载，清朝会稽周士芳曾结茅修炼于此。洞口下方有碧霄道院，清初已废圮，如今只见墙垣遗址。

　　大仰峰和中仰峰，少有人去。一是山高路远，想登临其巅并非易事，能亲身到此的人也就不多了；二是大仰和中仰风景平平，在小仰峰的碧霄洞已能得武夷最高处的妙境，也就不必再劳心费力了。

Seventh Bend

Glide the boat to the green beach at the seventh bend;

Glance back at Yinping Peak and Xianzhang Peak.

It's a pity there was rain last night,

Even the cliffside spring is cold.

◎ 三仰峰。（郑友裕 摄）
Sanyang Peak. (Photo by Zheng Youyu)

■ Sanyang Peak (Three Peaks Upwards)

Sanyang Peak is the highest peak in Wuyishan National Scenic Area and sits to the north of the seventh bend. Three peaks overlap—the highest one is Dayang (Big) Peak; the middle one is Zhongyang (Middle) Peak; the lowest one is Xiaoyang (Small) Peak. The tops of the peaks all face the east. Seen from the top of Sanyang Peak, Mount Wuyi peaks look like a pride of lions or a herd of running horses. Although Sanyang Peak is only 700 meters above sea level, it can be seen from (almost) everywhere. Ni Tianhan in the Qing Dynasty wrote a poem to praise Sanyang Peak.

Three peaks are inserted from the sky,

Which are cold during the day and covered by the green shade;

Stone paths are mostly newly carved,

The well spring is still gushing old cinnabar;

The trees in the cloud being lush green,

Many pieces of red clouds flow in the cave hole;

There are no unsightly things in this deep place,

Spring often smiles on the peach blossom.

"The well spring is still gushing old cinnabar" and "many pieces of red clouds flow in the cave hole" describe Xiaoyang Peak. There is Bixiao Cave at the mid-level and above the cave there is the inscription "Wuyi's Highest Point" written by Lin Pei in the Ming Dynasty. According to legend, it was Bai Yuchan's alchemy well beside the cave. It is recorded that Zhou Shifang in the Qing Dynasty built a small hut and sought enlightenment here. Under the cave there is the Bixiao Taoist Temple, but it was ruined in the early years of the Qing Dynasty. Now you can only see the ruins of the wall. But remember, once, long ago … the immortals practiced here.

Few people go to Dayang Peak and Zhongyang Peak mostly because the mountain is high and the road is long. And the landscapes of the two peaks are ordinary. Bixiao Cave in the Xiaoyang Peak has the best view, so don't waste the strength to climb the other two peaks.

© 三仰峰最高处。（宋春 摄）
"Wuyi's Highest Point" at Sanyang Peak (Photo by Song Chun)

八曲

八曲风烟势欲开，

鼓楼岩下水潆洄；

莫言此处无佳景，

自是游人不上来。

■ 鼓子峰

　　八曲滩浅水急，鼓子峰双峰骈立，朝云出岫时如一枝并蒂金莲，映耀碧空。这里有令人目不暇接的怪石、灵芝石、观音石、品岩石、上水狮石、大小廪石、上下水龟石等参差错落，争奇斗巧。人至此处，观赏山石，浮想联翩。

Eighth Bend

The wind and clouds at the eighth bend are about to open,

Water swirls around Gulou Rock;

Do not say there is no good scenery here.

Just because tourists can't come up here.

◎ 梅拥并莲。（郑友裕 摄）

The twin lotus attended by the plum blossom. (Photo by Zheng Youyu)

■ Guzi Peak

The eighth bend has shallow water and riffles, with two peaks (Guzi Peak) rising together like golden twin lotus flowers on one stalk as the sun shines on the mountains. There are a variety of unique stones around this place, such as Ganoderma Stone, Guanyin Stone, Pinyan Rock, Shangshui Lion Stone, Granary Stones of All Sizes, Shangxia Turtle Stone and others. They are all uneven and strewn about in random, with different shapes. Tourists here, watching the rocks, can imagine a lot of things.

九曲

九曲将穷眼豁然，

桑麻雨露见平川；

渔郎更觅桃源路，

除是人间别有天。

■ 白云峰

九曲尽头水势平缓，山水相接处是白云峰。至此，放眼西望，豁然开朗是平川。所以自古便有人以"平川"作为九曲码头所在地星村的雅称。

白云峰又名灵峰，盘亘在溪北，与大王峰分别守在九曲溪的两端。每当拂晓，常有白云在这座耸峙于九曲之尾的奇峰腰际飘荡，聚散分合，变幻无穷。峰峦在云雾里若隐若现，宛若海上仙山，是观看日出云海之佳所。

白云峰的峰腰有白云禅寺。在九曲漂游时骋目北望，可以看到盘踞在溪北白云岩的这座古寺庙。寺庙傍崖临溪而建，状若悬空。若要亲自探访，需通过星村大桥，顺山路向东北而行，抵达白云岩山麓，再拾级而上。

■ Baiyun (Cloud) Peak

By the end of the ninth bend, the water flow is gentle, wrapping around Baiyun (White Cloud) Peak. From here, looking west, you see a flat plain. Since ancient times, it's been called "Pingchuan (Plain)"—Xingcun Township and the ninth bend pier are located here.

Baiyun Peak, also known as Ling Peak, lying to the north of the stream, and Great King Peak to the south keep watch at the two sides of Nine-Bend Stream. At dawn, there are often white clouds drifting around the mountain's waist, getting together and then dispersing again creating infinite forms. Sometimes Baiyun Peak is hidden in the clouds, like the fairy mountains of the sea—in ancient Chinese fairy tales the gods lived on mountains in the Eastern Sea—This is also a good place to watch the sunrise amidst the clouds.

At the waist of Baiyun Peak there is Baiyun Zen Temple. If you look into the distance to the north while floating on Nine-Bend Stream, you can see the ancient temple wedged in Baiyun Rock to the north of the stream. The temple was built on the side of the cliff, overlooking the stream, as if suspended between heaven and earth. If you want to visit it, you need to cross the bridge at Xing Village, travel along the mountain pathway to the northeast, and when you reach the foot of Baiyun Rock, climb the stairs.

◎ 九曲尽头。（郑友裕 摄）

The end of the ninth bend. (Photo by Zheng Youyu)

Ninth Bend

The ninth bend is the last stop for your eyes,

Crops, rain and dew on the plain;

The fisherman wants to find the way to Taoyuan,

Is there another heaven outside this world?

白云禅寺的前身是有1,500多年历史的白云庵，至今仍是一块清净空灵之地，去往这里的路上只有少数的本地茶农和摄影爱好者，少见游客。你可以到寺里歇脚喝茶，品尝一顿只需按心随喜、添点香油钱的斋饭，也可继续向上，通过一段需要借助绳子攀爬的陡路，直到白云岩顶的御仙台。

在此南望九曲上游，溪流飘然如带，山水皆收眼底。中国现代作家郁达夫曾有诗作："武夷三十六雄峰，九曲清溪境不同。山水若从奇处看，西湖终是小家容。"站在白云岩峰顶，再三品味这九曲画廊，顿感此言不虚。

在白云岩峰北尽头，有一轩敞岩洞，名曰极乐国，传为修行之地。进洞之路十分危险，上下都是绝壁，壁间只有一线横坳，必须要俯身蛇形，盘壁而过，方能进入。赶上雨天，静坐于此，云雾就在你眼前飘过，雨帘落下，还真会生出歌曲《侠客行》里的念头："办些许该做的事，任人吵闹喧腾，不必听，遂了初心，拂衣便走，且把此生藏人海，埋没我的姓名。"

通往极乐国的路没有防护，太过危险，不建议游客前往，留一丝遗憾吧，这才是真正的圆满。

◎ 远眺白云峰和白云禅寺。（彭善安 摄）
Baiyun Peak and Baiyun Zen Temple seen from a distance. (Photo by Peng Shan'an)

Baiyun Zen Temple, formerly known as Baiyun Monastery with a history of over 1,500 years, is still a special spiritual place. On the way to the temple, you may come across a few local tea farmers, some photography enthusiasts, and a few wandering tourists. You can go to the temple to have a cup of tea, enjoy a vegetarian meal and just donate money at your discretion for their candles and oil … and then continue up the steep path to Yuxian Platform on top of Baiyun Rock … with the help of a rope.

Now rest and relax for a moment and look southward at the upstream of Nine-Bend Stream. It is like a floating jeweled belt snaking around the mountains, with the panoramic view filling your eyes. Yu Dafu, a modern Chinese writer, wrote a poem:"Mount Wuyi's thirty-six peaks and nine bends are all different. If you look at the Mount Wuyi landscape this way, West Lake (in Hangzhou) is like a small pond." Standing on top of Baiyun Rock, continuously savoring the gallery of nine bends scenes, suddenly you will understand and agree that this is true.

At the north end of Baiyun Rock, there is an open cave known as the Kingdom of Bliss. It is said to be a place where the Taoists sought enlightenment long ago. The pathway into the cave is very dangerous. At the top and the bottom are cliffs, and there's only a horizontal cut between the rock walls, so you have to bend down in a snake-like position, and climb over the rock if you want to enter the place. On a rainy day, just sit quietly inside here, clouds and mist floating in front of your eyes, a curtain of rain falling before you—and listen to the words of the old song:

> Do some things that should be done;
> Don't care about the noisy world.
> Don't listen to others;
> Follow my original heart.
> Flick the sleeve then go;
> Hide my life from the crowd,
> And forget all names.

Unfortunately, the pathway to the Kingdom of Bliss is unprotected and too dangerous to be recommended for tourists.

茶区中心的风景线

■ 三坑两涧

武夷山不独以山水之奇而奇，更以茶产之奇而奇。

武夷山碧水丹山的独特自然环境所孕育的武夷岩茶，有着"岩骨花香"的优秀品质。耳熟能详的三坑两涧为武夷岩茶核心产区，所产武夷岩茶品质极佳，古时所谓"正岩茶"也多产于此处。著名的茶区不但茶为上品，风景也是秀丽之中有奇伟之气。正所谓：名山出名茶，名茶耀名山。

三坑两涧指的是慧苑坑、牛栏坑、大坑口、流香涧和悟源涧。"三坑"中慧苑坑最长，牛栏坑宽而短，大坑口在牛栏坑的南面。"两涧"中的流香涧位于慧苑坑南侧，至慧苑坑汇入章堂涧；悟源涧位于马头岩南侧，是流经马鞍岩与马头岩之间的一条涧水，至马头岩之南汇入三姑涧。

Scenery at the Center of the Tea Production Area

■ Three Pits and Two Ravines

Mount Wuyi is not only unique in its landscape, but also in the matchless flavour of its tea.

The unique natural environment breeds Wuyi Rock Tea, which has the excellent quality of "rock bone and flower fragrance". The familiar Three-Pit and Two-Ravine area, which produces Wuyi Rock Tea of the highest quality, is the core producing area of Wuyi Rock Tea. The ancient so-called "real rock tea" was from here, too. This area is famous not only for its excellent tea, but also for its scenic beauty. This is why you'll often hear: "Famous tea produced from beautiful mountains adds more glory to the beautiful mountains."

The Three-Pit and Two-Ravine area refers to Huiyuan Pit, Niulan Pit, Big Pit, Liuxiang Ravine and Wuyuan Ravine. Huiyuan Pit is the longest, Niulan Pit is wide and short, and Big Pit lies to the south of Niulan Pit. Liuxiang Ravine is located on the south side of Huiyuan Pit and joins Zhangtang Stream when it flows through Huiyuan Pit. Wuyuan Ravine is located on the south side of Horse Head Rock. It is between Maan Rock and Horse Head Rock and flows into Sangu Stream at the south of Horse Head Rock. (You don't need to memorize this—just enjoy the tea from this area.)

◎ 悟源涧。（郑友裕 摄）
Wuyuan Ravine. (Photo by Zheng Youyu)

　　三坑两涧岩谷之间峭峰林立，幽涧叮咚，雨雾氤氲。由于岩崖和森林的遮蔽，这里的日照时间在4至6个小时之间，夏季以漫射光为主，对于茶树的生长恰到好处。岩坑之中土质疏松，砂砾含量较高，通气（水）性好，富含钾、锰，酸度适中，也为茶树所喜。这里的地貌还有一个特点，就是岩石的质地松散，每逢下雨，雨水被岩缝吸收。雨过天晴阳光照耀时，岩壁就会由于热胀冷缩而发生轻微膨胀，挤出这些溶解了矿物质的雨水，被当地人称为"石乳"，石乳终年沿着岩壁流淌，滋养着山谷中的茶树。这样的地形地貌和微域气候构成了被称为"教科书式"的茶叶生长环境，孕育着独一无二的武夷岩茶。

The mountains and valleys between the Three-Pit and Two-Ravine have many peaks and mountain streams which make a pleasing rippling sound when it's raining. Shaded by rocky cliffs and forests, the sun only shines in here for four to six hours during the day, and even the summer is dominated by a diffuse light, all of which makes it perfect for growing tea. In the pits, the soil is loose and contains a lot of sand and gravel, which provides good aeration and water drainage, rich in potassium, manganese, with moderate acidity—all are essential for superior tea. Besides, the rocks here have a loose texture and can absorb much rain water on rainy days. When the sun shines, the rocks swell slightly with heat and contract with cold. The mineral-dissolved rain, known locally as "stone milk", then flows through the crevices all year round and nourishes the tea trees in the valleys. Such landform and micro-climate make the best environment for growing tea—the unique Wuyi Rock Tea.

From the translator: Let me explain. Like wine making, the secret is balance—balance of wind, rain, sunshine, drainage, etc. All the elements in balance mean the best tea.

◎ 茶树春芽。（郑友裕 摄）
The spring buds of tea trees. (Photo by Zheng Youyu)

◎ 岩骨花香慢游道。（郑友裕 摄）
Rock Bone and Flower Fragrance Wandering Path. (Photo by Zheng Youyu)

■ 岩骨花香慢游道

　　岩骨花香慢游道穿行于武夷山核心产茶区，被戏称为武夷山茶区内最贵的一条道路。这条慢游道起于水帘洞，沿章堂涧而下，终于天心岩九龙窠，全程2.8千米，风景、人文俱佳。若在春季采茶时节来这里，果真是一路飘满茶香。这是团队游客不容易到达的地方，如果你爱茶、懂茶，或者仅仅是想了解武夷岩茶，那你一定要来这里走走，体会一下"岩韵"二字的由来。

Rock Bone and Flower Fragrance Wandering Path (Roaming Path)

The Rock Bone and Flower Fragrance Wandering Path winds through the core tea producing area of Mount Wuyi, which is referred to as the most expensive road in Mount Wuyi Scenic Area. This path starts from the Water Curtain Cave, winds along the Zhangtang Stream and then down to Jiulongke at Tianxin Rock, a 2.8-kilometer scenic and cultural journey. If you come here in the spring tea-picking season, the entire way is full of tea fragrance. It is not easy for large groups to reach this place; however, if you love tea, or just want to understand Wuyi Rock Tea, then you must come and walk here, to experience the special fragrance of this special tea.

◎ 九龙窠茶园。（郑友裕 摄）
The tea plantation at Jiulongke. (Photo by Zheng Youyu)

■ 天车架

自水帘洞路口拾级而下，会经过武夷山有名的古崖居遗址——丹霞嶂天车架，它嵌于崖壁半腰的岩罅中，洞口是木架结构的护栏。崖居是古代山民的一种居住形式，利用山体为屏障、岩穴为居所，既能防兽、防盗，又能节省材料。天车架相传为清咸丰年间当地乡绅为躲避战乱而建的避难所，建造时为节约时间，架天车（简单的机械起重装置）以运送材料。所建崖居为土木结构，恰如空中楼阁，东边为膳食区，瓮、石臼、舂杵、土灶等遗物均保存完好。中部是起居区，深广各数十米，为两层木楼房，梁、柱、檩俱在。西端有4部天车，应是当时载人及传送物资所用。各功能区之间还有木梯、栈道相连，形成一个完整的住宅群，当真是"螺蛳壳里做道场"。

■ Tianche (Sky Crane) Frame

Walk down from Water Curtain Cave, and you will pass Tianche Frame at Danxiazhang, a famous ancient cliff dwelling site in Mount Wuyi. It is embedded in a crack in the middle of a cliff; the entrance has a wooden guardrail. Cliff dwellings were popular with some ancient mountain people, where they used part of the mountain for the walls, and rock caves for their residence. These dwellings could keep out wild animals, guard against theft and save on materials. Legend has it that Tianche Frame was built during 1851—1861 in the Qing Dynasty as a shelter for local squires to avoid war. To save time during construction, Tianche (a simple mechanical lifting device) was used to lift materials up. The basic structure of a cliff dwelling is earth and wood, almost like a pavilion in the air. The east side of Tianche Frame is the dietary area, with urns, stone mortars, ground pestles, stoves and other remains still well preserved. The middle part is the living area, which is dozens of meters in depth and width, and two floors of wood planks, beams, columns, and purlin, all remaining there. At the western side, there are four Tianche devices, which were used for carrying people and materials to the dwelling. There are also wooden ladders and plank pathways connecting the functional areas to form a complete residential zone, whch indeed shows "building a home in a seashell".

天车架。（郑友裕 摄）
Tianche Frame. (Photo by Zheng Youyu)

◎ 鹰嘴岩。（郑友裕 摄）
Eagle Mouth Rock. (Photo by Zheng Youyu)

■ 鹰嘴岩

　　继续漫步，来到鹰嘴岩，这里因石形似雄鹰展翅欲飞而得名。鹰嘴岩一端向前突出，尖曲如鹰嘴，光秃秃的岩顶生长着一株遒劲的古老刺柏。从岩顶直削而下的岩壁白里透红，而微微拱起的岩脊却是一片苍黑，宛若雄鹰之翼。

　　石桥边有两株梅树，梅花开时，便是赏梅的好去处。

　　山路一转，即可抵达慧苑禅寺。禅寺始建于宋代，朱熹曾到此游历，留下了"静我神"匾额。远眺寺院，错落的马头墙高低有序，寺前小桥流水，十分秀美。慧苑坑一带的茶园出产多种武夷名丛，记载中有白鸡冠、铁罗汉、水仙等。慧苑寺曾有茶厂数家，收入颇丰。

Eagle Mouth Rock

Continue your walk to Eagle Mouth Rock. The rock here is shaped like an eagle flapping its wings about to fly, hence its name. One side of Eagle Mouth Rock protrudes in front, curved like an eagle's mouth. On the top of the bare rock grows an ancient juniper. The white and red palisades are straight from the top, while the gently arched side slopes are black, forming the eagle's wings.

There are two winter plum trees on the side of the stone bridge. When they blossom, it is a good place to enjoy the winter sweet fragrances.

Turn onto the mountain path, and you can reach Huiyuan Temple. It was built in the Song Dynasty. Zhu Xi traveled here once, leaving a plaque "Jing Wo Shen (Calm down my spirit)". Overlooking the temple from a distance, the undulating horsehead walls, the delicate bridge and the flowing stream make a very beautiful setting. The tea plantations in Huiyuan Pit produce a variety of Wuyi famous teas, including Baijiguan (White Cockscomb), Tieluohan (Iron Arhat) and Shuixian (Daffodil). Huiyuan Temple also used to have a number of lucrative tea factories.

◎ 慧苑禅寺。（郑友裕 摄）
Huiyuan Temple. (Photo by Zheng Youyu)

■ 大红袍母树

过双悟石桥，左转，流香涧便现于眼前。由于特殊的地貌发育和流水侵蚀作用的影响，流香涧两侧石壁直立如墙，两相对峙，峡谷宽度仅一米多，窄如小巷。人行此处，涧水潺潺，山风拂面，清凉惬意。

出流香涧东行，沿茶园间的石径翻过好汉坡的小山岗，即进入九龙窠，这里有驰名中外的大红袍母树，生长于悬崖峭壁的石基上，已有300多年的历史。在这个天下闻名之处驻足凝望，你会有机会听到身边导游们风格不一的解说词，尤其是"半壁江山"的故事。

■ The Mother Trees of Dahongpao

Cross Shuangwu Stone Bridge, turn left, and Liuxiang Ravine is in front of you. Due to the special geomorphologic development and erosion effect of flowing water, the two sides of Liuxiang Ravine are upright like walls facing each other. The ravine is only about one meter wide and narrow like a path. When you walk here with the gurgling stream and mountain breeze, it is very cool and comfortable.

Going out east from Liuxiang Ravine, climb over the small hill Haohan (Hero) Slope along the stone path between tea plantations, and you will get to the Jiulongke—here you can see the world-famous Mother Trees of Dahongpao, which grow on a stone foundation in the cliff. They have a history of more than 300 years. Pause and look at these world-famous trees; you may have the opportunity to hear different commentaries from different tour guides around you, especially the story of "half of the country".

© 流香洞。（郑友裕 摄）
Liuxiang Ravine. (Photo by Zheng Youyu)

◎ 大红袍鲜叶。（郑友裕 摄）
The fresh tea leaves of Dahongpao. (Photo by Zheng Youyu)

　　1972年中美建交之时，美国总统尼克松访华，毛泽东主席送给他四两（200克）武夷山大红袍母树所产的茶叶，这个数量让尼克松总统颇感意外。周恩来总理心思通透，从旁解释道："总统先生，主席把'半壁江山'都送给您了！"并道出其中缘由。原来大红袍母树因着细小甘泉及藓类有机物的常年滋养，所产茶叶天赋不凡，冲至九泡仍不失真味，为"茶中王者"，然而此等珍品，一年产量却只有八两（400克），堪称国宝，是中国历代皇家贡品。奉送一半，正好是"半壁江山"，如此成就了一段"大红袍外交"的佳话。

◎ 大红袍母树。（郑友裕 摄）

The Mother Trees of Dahongpao. (Photo by Zheng Youyu)

In 1972, when the two countries established diplomatic relations, the US President Richard Nixon visited China and Chairman Mao Zedong gave him 200 grams of tea from Mother Trees of Dahongpao in Mount Wuyi as a present. Premier Zhou Enlai said, "Mr President, the Chairman has given you 'half of the country'!" and explained why. Because of the extraordinary nature of this tea produced by the constant nourishment of tiny sweet springs and moss organisms, you can reuse one portion nine times and it doesn't lose its original taste, so it is the "king of tea". However, the annual output of these trees is only 400 grams, which makes it a national treasure as it was a tribute to the imperial family in all dynasties of China. So giving away 200 grams (half of the annual output) as a gift is exactly like "half of the country's treasure". This made a good story about "Dahongpao diplomacy".

如今，大红袍母树已作为古树名木列入武夷山世界文化与自然遗产名录。2003年，武夷山市政府为大红袍母树投了保额为一亿元人民币的保险。2006年起，武夷山市政府对大红袍母树实行特别管护，限制采摘，确保其生长良好，并严格保护周边的生态环境。看到这里，你或许会"望树兴叹"，不过不用遗憾，早在20世纪80年代，大红袍母树的无性繁殖就取得了成功，扦插成活的枝条所产的茶叶传承了母树完整的"岩骨花香"，使珍稀贡品大红袍得以飞入寻常百姓家。不过，人工繁殖和培育大红袍由梦想变为现实，是经过了20多年的尝试与努力，由大红袍之父陈德华先生完成，那又是一个人与自然亲密相处、互相成就的故事。

Today, the Mother Trees of Dahongpao have been included as famous ancient trees of the world cultural and natural heritage list for Mount Wuyi. In 2003, the Wuyishan municipal government insured the mother trees for 100 million yuan. Since 2006, the Wuyishan municipal government has implemented special management and protection for the mother trees, restricting the picking to ensure its good growth and strictly protecting the surrounding ecological environment. Seeing this, you may "look at the trees and sigh", but don't feel sad about it. As early as in the 1980s, the asexual grafting of the Dahongpao mother trees achieved success, and the tea produced from the new cuttings inherited all the characteristics of the mother trees enabling this rare tribute tea to enter into ordinary people's homes. However, it took more than 20 years of efforts to realize the dream of cloning and cultivating Dahongpao. This was achieved by "the father of Dahongpao", Chen Dehua, which is another story of man and nature working together for mutual benefit.

◎ 大红袍之父、武夷岩茶（大红袍）制作技艺传承人陈德华。（郑友裕 摄）

Chen Dehua, father of Dahongpao and inheritor of Wuyi Rock Tea (Dahongpao) producing techniques. (Photo by Zheng Youyu)

古人说武夷山"山中土气宜茶",今天时髦的说法就是"风土",指土壤类型、地形、地理位置、光照条件、降水量、昼夜温差和微生物环境等影响茶叶风味的自然因素。在山中行走,四时流转入眼入心,遇上老茶树,细细观察,会发现茶树生长得内敛、收摄、独立,缓慢而有节奏,对周边环境顺纳、适应,与之共生,达到平衡和谐的境界。

穿行于岩骨花香慢游道,风土秘密和久远传奇蕴藏其间,你能感受到的远远胜于语言所能表达的。

看过大红袍母树,听完"半壁江山"故事,不妨再去大红袍祖庭感受禅茶一味。

Ancient people said that Mount Wuyi is "suitable for tea due to the local climate". Today, the fashionable term is "terroir" (the same word the French use for their famous vineyards), which refers to the natural factors that affect tea flavor, such as soil type, topography, geographical location, sunlight, precipitation, temperature difference between day and night, etc.—the entire microbial environment. When walking in the mountains, you will see the old tea trees in your eyes and feel them in your heart. If you carefully observe them, you will find that the tea trees grow in a restrained manner, i.e. absorbing, independently, in a slow rhythmic cycle. They conform to the surrounding environment, live within it, and maintain a state of balance and harmony.

As you walk slowly through the paths, learning the secret of the land and the legends of the past, you often "feel" more than words can express.

After seeing Mother Trees of Dahongpao and listening to the story about "half of the country", you should go to Dahongpao Ancestral Temple to enjoy "Zentea"—and notice the similarity between the Zen culture and the tea culture.

© 章堂洞风光。（宋春 摄）
The scenery at Zhangtang Ravine. (Photo by Song Chun)

■ 大红袍祖庭

大红袍祖庭位于天心岩下的天心永乐禅寺，建有茶祖殿和大红袍祖庭纪念碑。据《武夷山志》记载，天心永乐禅寺前身为山心庵，曾是武夷山最大的佛教寺院。唐乾符元年（874）中秋之夜，扣冰古佛在此望天心圆月而开悟，留下"天心明月"这个著名的禅学公案，后人有感于扣冰古佛的禅学境界，便把山心庵改名为天心庵。

传说明洪武十八年（1385），举子丁显赴京赶考，途经武夷山时患疾，卧床不起，被天心庵僧人搭救，并以茶入药治疗。丁显后中状元，再访武夷山谢恩，方才得知治好自己的是九龙窠几株茶树所产的茶叶，于是深信该茶可以治病，便带了一些回京进贡。恰逢皇后生病，百药无效，丁显献上此茶，皇后饮之，果然得以康复。皇上龙颜大悦，赐红袍一件，命状元亲自前往武夷山九龙窠，披在茶树上以示龙恩，并派人看护，年年采制茶叶，悉数进贡。从此，这几株茶树便以"大红袍"之名扬名天下。

■ Dahongpao Ancestral Temple

Dahongpao Ancestral Temple is located in Tianxin Yongle Zen Temple under Tianxin Rock. According to *Records of Mount Wuyi*, Tianxin Yongle Zen Temple, formerly known as Shanxin Monastery, was once the largest Buddhist temple in the Mount Wuyi area. During the Mid-Autumn Festival night in 874, Koubing, an ancient Buddhist master was here looking at the heaven and moon when he realized enlightenment, sparking the famous Zen koan "the moon in the heart of the sky". In order to memorialize the enlightenment of Koubing, the locals later changed the temple's name to Tianxin Monastery.

According to legend, in 1385 of the Ming Dynasty, a candidate named Ding Xian went to the capital for the imperial examination. When he passed through Mount Wuyi, he became ill and bedridden; fortunately, he was nursed back to good health by the monks of Tianxin Monastery and treated with their tea as medicine. Afterwards he ranked first in the exam and returned to Mount Wuyi to thank the monks for their help and learned that the tea was produced from a few tea trees in Jiulongke. He reasoned that the tea could work wonders, so he took some back to the capital as tribute. Later the queen got ill and all the drugs were ineffective. Ding Xian presented this tea, the queen drank it, and recovered from the illness. The emperor was very happy, so he ordered Ding Xian to go personally to Jiulongke and drape a red robe on the tea trees to show the dragon throne's grace. The emperor also sent people to look after the trees and pick tea leaves to make tribute tea annually. From then on, these few tea plants became known as "Dahongpao (Big Red Robe)".

◎ 天心永乐禅寺旧殿。（郑友裕 摄）
The old building of Tianxin Yongle Zen Temple. (Photo by Zheng Youyu)

　　天心岩地处山北风景区，位置居中，四通八达。从这里往东，可到杜辖岩、神通岩和盘珠岩；往西，可到九龙窠、流香涧、清凉峡、玉柱峰和慧苑岩；往南，可到三花峰、马头岩和磊石岩，进而可穿过悟源涧抵天游峰览胜；往北，可到火焰峰、丹霞峰、鹰嘴岩和水帘洞，到了水帘洞，还可以去到青狮岩、佛国岩、龙峰和莲花峰探幽，由此可知天心岩在山中所处地位——山之心。

　　于武夷山景区内行走，天心永乐禅寺可作为中午休息的落脚点，午饭于寺中过斋，餐费随喜。若赶上佛教节日，又会多些不一样的体验。比如四月初八浴佛日，武夷山地区有吃黑米饭的习俗。黑米饭并非用黑米煮成，而是把糯米用乌饭树的汁液浸泡后蒸熟而成，据说与释迦牟尼的弟子目连救母的传说有关。民间在这一日也会举行与孝道相关的活动。

Tianxin Rock is located in the middle of North Mountain scenic area, extending in all directions. From here to the east, you can reach Duxia Rock, Shentong Rock and Panzhu Rock. To the west, you can go to Jiulongke, Liuxiang Ravine, Qingliang (Cool) Gorge, Yuzhu Peak and Huiyuan Rock. To the south, you can reach Sanhua (Three Flowers) Peak, Horse Head Rock and Leishi Rock, and also climb to the top of Tianyou Peak through Wuyuan Stream. To the north, you can go to Huoyan (Flame) Peak, Danxia Peak, Eagle Mouth Rock and Water Curtain Cave, and you can also go to Qingshi (Blue Lion) Rock, Foguo (Buddhist Land) Rock, Long (Dragon) Peak and Lianhua (Lotus) Peak for more exploration. Therefore you can see that Tianxin Rock is centered in the heart of the mountains.

Traveling through Mount Wuyi Scenic Area, Tianxin Yongle Zen Temple can be used as a rest stop at noontime—you can enjoy the vegetarian lunch in the temple—just pay at your own discretion. If you catch a Buddhist festival, you will have an additional wonderful experience. For example, during the Buddha Bathing Day on April 8th of the lunar calendar, it is the custom to eat black rice in Mount Wuyi. Black rice is not cooked black rice, but it is steamed glutinous rice pre-soaked in the juice of the black rice tree. It is said to be related to the legend of Sakyamuni's disciple Mulian who saved his mother. Folk activities related to filial piety are also held on this day.

◎ 天心永乐禅寺新大殿。（郑友裕 摄）
The main hall of Tianxin Yongle Zen Temple. (Photo by Zheng Youyu)

◎ 蜡烛会上的青草药。（宋春 摄）

The herbal medicines at Candle Festival. (Photo by Song Chun)

　　武夷山家喻户晓的传统民俗活动——蜡烛会，则是为了纪念扣冰古佛。蜡烛会起源于唐朝，历史悠久。它以崇安（今武夷山市）北路乡民迎扣冰古佛为背景，每到农历二月，蜡烛会活动自吴屯、黎口、岚谷、大浑等北面乡村开始，几乎贯穿整个月。乡民迎请扣冰古佛，烧蜡烛，以禳疫除灾。在各地的蜡烛会中，以武夷山市区城关（农历二月廿一日）的最为隆重。

　　如今，武夷山市蜡烛会已发展成为传统手工艺产品、中草药等的交易盛会之一，其规模和影响堪称闽北之最。每到会期，人涌如潮。你可以在这里看到各种乡村土特产，特别是青草药、农具、日用家具等。

The Candle Festival, a well-known traditional folk activity in Mount Wuyi, is held in memory of master Koubing. The festival originated in the Tang Dynasty and has a long history. It took place in Chongan (today's Wuyishan City) when the villagers in the northern area welcomed the ancient Buddha Koubing. Every February of the lunar calendar, the Candle Festival activities begin from Wutun, Likou, Langu, Dahun and other northern villages, and last almost throughout all of February. Villagers invite Koubing Buddha with burning candles to ward off diseases and disasters. The most solemn candle ceremony is in the urban area of the city (on the 21st day of the second lunar month).

Nowadays, the Candle Festival in Wuyishan City has developed into one of the biggest market days for traditional handicraft products and Chinese herbal medicines—maybe the largest such market in northern Fujian. Every time the festival is held, people flock to enjoy the event. You can see all kinds of local products here, especially fresh herbal medicine, farm tools, daily items and more.

◎ 挑选草药的老人。（宋春 摄）
An old woman selecting herbs. (Photo by Song Chun)

■ 牛栏坑

自天心禅寺舍利塔旁的一小路下行，可至牛栏坑。如今，单单说"核心产区"已不足以体现牛栏坑的知名与热度，你甚至可以叫它"当红小生"。前人盛誉武夷岩茶"臻山川精英秀气所钟，品具岩骨花香之胜"，来到这里便可仔细体会。

茶树喜爱阴湿的自然环境，牛栏坑经常云雾弥漫，恰好适宜茶树生长。"盆栽式茶园"在这里随处可见，这也是武夷岩茶栽种的独特之处。

牛栏坑内的摩崖石刻"不可思议"，与武夷名丛水金龟有关。古时天心禅寺有一株长于牛栏坑岩边的名丛，名曰"水金龟"。有一日大雨倾盆，茶园崩塌，水金龟随泥石滑到峰下牛栏坑中。坑中地块属兰谷岩茶厂，茶厂工人便以石护之，精心管理。此后两家为争此株，历讼公堂，耗资千金。水金龟随之名声大振。学者施棱先生闻之，大惑不解，于是在其旁题勒"不可思议"，以抒感叹。

■ Niulan Pit

Walking down the path beside the stupa at Tianxin Zen Temple, you can reach Niulan Pit. Actually, "core area of production" is not sufficient to describe the fame and popularity of Niulan Pit—you probably should call it the "super star" tea producing area of Mount Wuyi. You will be able to understand the high reputation of Wuyi Rock Tea better after you come here.

Tea trees like a wet natural environment, and mist and fog often fill this pit, making it perfectly suitable for the growth of high-quality tea trees. The "potted tea plantation" style planting can be seen everywhere here (rock walls holding the soil in place), which is a unique feature of rock tea plantations in Mount Wuyi.

Niulan Pit cliff stone inscription "Incredible" is related to one of the famous teas in Mount Wuyi called Shuijingui (Golden Water Turtle). In ancient times, Tianxin Zen Temple had this famous tea tree that grew on the edge of Niulan Pit. One day, when it was raining heavily, a wall collapsed, and the tea tree, along with mud and stones slid down to a lower part. However, the land in the lower part of the pit belonged to a different tea factory, Langu Rock Tea Factory, and the workers there protected this tea tree with stone walls and took good care of it. Later the two factories argued because of the new location of the tea tree, and finally litigated in court, costing a lot of money. Subsequently the tea became famous. Shi Leng, a scholar, heard about this and was puzzled, so he wrote "Incredible" to express his feelings.

○ 牛栏坑茶园。（郑友裕 摄）
The tea plantation at Niulan Pit. (Photo by Zheng Jouyu)

■ 马头岩

天心产区内还有马头岩，喜好武夷岩茶的人都知道这个山场的茶好，故有人称之为"与牛栏坑一时瑜亮的产茶区"。茶人口中的"马肉""牛肉"，分别指的就是马头岩和牛栏坑的肉桂。

马头岩五石骈列，形似马头，势如骏马奔腾，故也有"五马奔槽"的雅称。北有三花峰，似三朵盛开的巨花。附近有马鞍岩、铁郎寨、悟源涧等自然之所，又有磊石道观、凝云庵遗址等人文景观。游至此处，参访磊石道观的人多，旁边的凝云庵遗址，知道的人却寥寥。

据记载，这里"虽秋冬若夏春"，乃一福地。明代时，这里称为凝云庵、凝庵；清代时，改名为凝云道院。清代董天工《武夷山志》有记载：

"马头岩下，亦称凝庵。从换骨岩纤曲以入，中复夷旷，茂林修竹掩映左右，桃杏梅桂次第迭开。隆庆初，道士张德恩建，内有凝云阁、息机窝、鸣球亭、涌翠台。又从岩巅浚飞泉注莲池，曲水流觞以娱客，有巨石如几，可弈棋，勒'橘隐'二字，名橘隐石。景物佳胜，人谓之小蓬莱，今废。"

■ Matou (Horse Head) Rock

Matou Rock is in Tianxin tea plantation area. People who like Wuyi Rock Tea all know that the tea from this mountain field is so great that you can't tell which tea is better if compared with the tea from Niulan Pit. What people call "Marou" and "Niurou" respectively refer to the tea from Matou Rock and Niulan Pit.

There are five large stones in a row on Horse Head Rock, shaped like horses running. So they are called "five horses running to the trough". There is Sanhua Peak in the north, like three giant flowers in bloom. Nearby, there are Ma'an Rock, Tielang Village, Wuyuan Ravine and other natural scenic spots, as well as Leishi Taoist Temple, Ningyun Monastery Ruins and other cultural heritage sites. Many people will visit Leishi Taoist Temple, but few people know the Ningyun Monastery site next to it.

In the histories it is said, "Although it is autumn and winter elsewhere, the weather here is moderate and pleasant." People consider it a blessed place. In the Ming Dynasty, they called it Ningyun Monastery or Ning Monastery; and then in the Qing Dynasty, they renamed it Ningyun Taoist Temple. This is how it is recorded in Dong Tiangong's *Records of Mount Wuyi*:

"Ningyun Monastery, also Ning Monastery, lies under Horse Head Rock. You enter the area passing by Huangu Rock into an open space in the middle, surrounded by dense forest and bamboo trees. There are peach, apricot, and plum trees and also Osmanthus blossoms during different seasons. During 1567—1572, Taoist Zhang De'en built Ningyun Pavilion, Xiji Nest, Mingqiu Pavilion, and Yongcui Platform. The stream water flows into the lotus pool from the top of the rocks and swirls around the lotus flowers to entertain visitors. There is also a table-shaped boulder carved "Ju Yin", where people played chess games, so it got the name of Juyin Stone. With the beautiful scenery, people called the Ningyun Monastery area Small Penglai (Immortals' Island) before, but unfortunately now it has mostly been destroyed."

◎ 马头岩春色。（郑友裕 摄）
Horse Head Rock in spring. (Photo by Zheng Youyu)

◎ 凝云庵遗址。（宋春 摄）
The relics of Ningyun Monastery. (Photo by Song Chun)

关于凝云庵，从为数不多的资料中，可以想象出其在明代的辉煌鼎盛。明代吴立中有一首诗名为《游凝云庵》，写其"石楼高结万山阴"，这是何等的气势与气派；邱云霄的《寿凝庵张道人》里则有"鹿遇寻常径"的句子，反映出当时的生态与野趣。如今遇到鹿有困难，不过运气好的话，还是能看到白鹇出没的。

林则徐曾游览武夷山，为马头岩凝云庵题"积翠涵养"四字。依这四字，当知该处曾是草木繁茂、翠色重叠、修身养性之佳地。如今能看到的只是残败断石、颓废地基、疯狂生长的蔓草和凌乱的枯枝黄叶，简陋的棚内供奉着三皇元君的神位。路旁有一石，上可见"高冈独立"字样摩崖石刻。

"仙遗蝉蜕去，人问马头来"，遗址也好，圣地也罢，重要的是我们借此知道有那样一个人或一群人，曾经在此处修行、得道，后人纪念传颂，使他们的故事流传于世。这大自然中，这土、这水、这树、这石延续和传递着千百年的讯息，与之对话，你或许就可以在心中描摹出一幅仙台古亭、高空明月、清明淡泊的饮茶图来。

From just a few ancient records, we can imagine the brilliant heyday of Ningyun Monastery during the Ming Dynasty. Wu Lizhong from the Ming Dynasty wrote a stylized poem which said, "High stone buildings (the temple) make the mountains dark". In Qiu Yunxiao's poem, there is a sentence of "Meet deer in the ordinary path", which reflects the ecological environment and outdoor fun during that time. The deer are scarce now, but with any luck, a silver pheasant can still be seen or heard.

Lin Zexu once visited Mount Wuyi and wrote four words, "Gathered green; nourish spirit", for Ningyun Monastery. We can learn from these words that it was an area of lush vegetation, with green colors overlapping and where you could cultivate benevolence and virtue. Now unfortunately, all that can be seen are just ruins of the stone foundation, plus a tangle of vines, messy branches, yellow leaves and a humble shed worshiping the Sanhuang Goddesses. By the roadway there is a stone, on which you can see the carved words "Solitary high mountain".

As the saying goes, "When a scholar achieves enlightenment, people come to Horse Head Rock (for news)." They went there because many scholars practiced at Horse Head Rock. They wanted to see which scholar had become an immortal, i.e. his physical body had been released. Whether it is an ordinary site or a holy place, the important thing is that we know that there were people who once practiced and found enlightenment here, and their stories have been passed on through the ages. All of nature, the earth, the water, the trees, the rocks continue to transmit messages through eternity. Listening to them, you may be able to trace a tea drinking picture in your heart at an ancient fairy pavilion, with the bright moon hanging in the sky.

© 武夷山白鹇。（郑友裕 摄）
The silver pheasant in Mount Wuyi. (Photo by Zheng Youyu)

◎ 三贤像。（郑友裕 摄）
The statues of the three sages. (Photo by Zheng Youyu)

■ 水帘洞

"千载儒释道，万古山水茶"，落在武夷山产茶核心区，水帘洞茶区是不可或缺的代表。

水帘洞位于章堂涧北峰岩中，藏在收敛的岩腰内，洞口斜敞，岩壁形似凹透镜，有近200米高，洞顶有两处飞泉倾泻下来，遇山风吹散，飘洒开来，在阳光的照耀下彩光闪耀，像璀璨珠帘垂落空中，所以此处又称珠帘洞。这里有明代题刻"水帘洞"，还有"活源"二字引人注目，是撷取于朱熹的七绝名句"问渠那得清如许，为有源头活水来"；而楹联石刻"古今晴檐终日雨，春秋花月一联珠"更是点睛之笔。

水帘洞不仅以风景取胜，还以武夷山道教圣地而闻名，曾有"唐曜洞天"的旧名。此外，这里建有一座三贤祠。宋代学者刘甫，崇安人，抗金将领刘衡之子，遵父嘱终身不仕，隐于武夷山水帘洞，读书著述。其师五夫里刘子翚和学兄朱熹曾多次到水帘洞，与他共探理学奥义，对这方"为有源头活水来"的胜地赞赏有加。师徒三人逝世后，门人在水帘洞建三贤祠，并竖像祀奉刘子翚、朱熹、刘甫，以纪念三位贤哲。

透过明亮的水晶珠幔，可观赏山中的盆景式茶园。这方弹丸之地，旧时却有三家茶厂，厂中出品的正岩水仙声誉很高，深得南洋华侨青睐。时至今日，这里依然是武夷岩茶的优良产地。

◎ 水帘洞摩崖石刻。（宋春 摄）

The cliff inscriptions at Water Curtain Cave. (Photo by Song Chun)

▓ Water Curtain Cave

Among all the core tea production areas of Mount Wuyi, Water Curtain Cave is a place worth mentioning.

It is located between the rocks of north Zhangtang Stream, hidden in the convergence of the rock waist, with an inclined opening and a rock wall shaped like concave lens, nearly 200 meters high. There are two springs pouring down from the top of the cave, and when the mountain winds blow, drops of water fly in the sky and twinkle in the sunshine, like a bright pearl curtain dropping through the air; thus this place is also known as the Pearl Curtain Cave. There are Ming Dynasty inscriptions "Water Curtain Cave" and "Source of the living water" which catch your eyes. The latter is taken from Zhu Xi's famous poem "Ask why the ditch is so clean, because the source has living water". There is also a pair of couplets serving as the punchline, "It has been raining under the eave from ancient times; a pearl curtain falls down before the flowers and under the moon no matter it's spring or autumn."

Water Curtain Cave is not only famous for its scenery, but also as a holy place of Taoism in Mount Wuyi. Also nearby there is the Temple of Three Sages. Song Dynasty scholar Liu Fu from Chongan, who was the son of General Liu Heng, followed his father's advice not to be an official and stayed in Water Curtain Cave, reading and writing. His teacher Liu Zihui and his senior apprentice Zhu Xi came here many times, exploring Neo-Confucianism with him, and they appreciated the restful nature here very much. After their death, their disciples built a temple here and erected statues to commemorate the three sages—Liu Zihui, Zhu Xi and Liu Fu.

Through the bright crystal pearl curtain, you can enjoy the bonsai-style tea plantation in these mountains. In the old days, there were three tea factories in this small area. Zhengyan Shuixian tea produced by these factories enjoyed a high reputation and was favored by overseas Chinese in Southeast Asia (Nanyang). Even now, it is still an excellent production area for Wuyi Rock Tea.

◎ 水帘洞茶园。（郑友裕 摄）
The tea plantation at Water Curtain Cave. (Photo by Zheng Youyu)

◎ 佛国岩。（郑国虎 摄）

Foguo (Buddhist Land) Rock. (Photo by Zheng Guohu)

武夷的两极——溪南绝景和山北胜境

武夷山的名胜古迹多集中在九曲溪一带，但溪南也有绝景，令人流连忘返，山北亦有胜境，可探丛林苍翠。如果把溪南和山北看作武夷山国家级风景名胜区的南北极，这溪南绝景与山北胜境的"两极"风光绝对值得一看。

溪南绝景位于九曲溪二曲南面，有一线天和上下虎啸；山北胜境聚集于风景区的西北部，有以白岩船棺为代表的古越文化景观，以及分布于莲花峰、佛国岩、弥陀岩、碧石岩间的佛寺，彰显佛教文化。

◎ 弥陀岩。（郑国虎 摄）

Mituo (Amitabha Buddha) Rock. (Photo by Zheng Guohu)

The Two Poles of Wuyi—Beautiful Scenery at South of the Stream and North of the Mountains

Most of the scenic spots and historic sites of Mount Wuyi are concentrated in the Nine-Bend Stream area, but there is also spectacular scenery to the south of the stream, which is so enticing that it makes people linger there and forget to return. Additionally, there are scenic spots to the north of the mountains, where one can even explore a verdant jungle. Therefore, South of the Stream and North of the Mountains are regarded as the south and north poles of Wuyishan National Scenic Area, both of which are definitely worth a visit.

South of the Stream is located to the south of the second bend of Nine-Bend Stream, where there is A Sliver of Sky and Tiger Roaring Rock. The scenic spots to the north of the mountains are mainly in the northwestern part of the scenic area, where the ancient Yue cultural landscape is represented by the boat-shaped coffins in Bai (White) Rock, and the Buddhist cultural landscape displayed by the Buddhist temples around Lianhua (Lotus) Peak, Foguo (Buddhist Land) Rock, Mituo (Amitabha Buddha) Rock and Bishi (Green Stone) Rock.

■ 一线天

九曲溪二曲南面的幽邃峡谷中有一座巍然挺立的巨石，长数百丈，高千仞，名曰"灵岩"。岩端倾斜而出，覆盖着三个相邻的岩洞：灵岩洞、风洞和伏羲洞，著名的一线天景观便是横贯此三洞。从伏羲洞进入，辗转曲折行至深处，抬头仰望，能看到岩顶裂开一罅，就像是被利斧劈开一样，宽度不足一尺，长约100米，从中漏进一线天光，不愧为"鬼斧神工之奇"。这种三洞并列、一线见天的奇特景观，其成因自然会有不少神话传说，事实上则是地壳运动和长年累月流水溶解侵蚀的结果。因为洞中最窄处宽度只有大约40厘米，所以常有游客开玩笑说这是个考验身材的地方。

如此幽暗潮湿的石罅是蝙蝠天然的家，洞中生活着稀有的白蝙蝠，虽然给空气中带来一些不好的气味，但也平添一份奇趣。因为"蝠"与"福"谐音，在中国传统文化中，蝙蝠是一种祥兽，如果你在洞中不慎被蝠粪击中，向导一定会笑着说这是你的"福分"。

◎ 一线天。（郑友裕 摄）

A Sliver of Sky. (Photo by Zheng Youyu)

◎ 风洞。（郑友裕 摄）

Wind Cave. (Photo by Zheng Youyu)

■ A Sliver of Sky

In the south gorge of the second bend of Nine-Bend Stream, there is a huge rock standing upright, "hundreds of meters long and high". It is called "Ling Rock". The rock slopes out and covers three adjacent caves: Ling Rock Cave, Feng (Wind) Cave and Fuxi Cave. The famous A Sliver of Sky goes through these three caves. If you enter from Fuxi Cave, wind down to the bottom, and then look up, you can see a crack less than a foot wide and about a hundred meters long on the top of the rock, just like it was cut open by a sharp axe. Once you see the sky light, you will agree that it looks worthy of the comment "extraordinary workmanship". This unique landscape with the three-hole juxtaposition and the sliver of sky above has many myths and legends pertaining to its origins. In reality, the sky light is the result of geological crustal movements and years of water erosion. Because the narrowest part of the cave is only about 40 centimeters wide, visitors often joke that it is a test of one's figure.

Also inside the cave live a flock of rare white bats. They bring a strange smell to the air, but also add a lot of adventure. In Chinese the sound of the word for bat (Bianfu) is similar to the word for blessing (Fu). So the bat is regarded as a kind of auspicious animal. If you are accidentally hit by bat dung in the cave, the guide will smile and say it is your "good fortune".

◎ 虎啸岩。（郑友裕 摄）

Tiger Roaring Rock. (Photo by Zheng Youyu)

■ 虎啸岩

　　虎啸岩盘踞在一线天北面，是溪南第一胜景，得此名是因为半壁有一巨洞，山风吹过，声若虎啸，威震群山。虎啸岩四面陡峭，巍然而立，可赏怪石灵泉之天趣，天成禅院、语儿泉等虎啸八景就分布在这巨大的山岩之上，若想一一登临，有一条直贴崖壁的好汉坡之路可以挑战，据说比天游峰还要陡峭。

　　天成禅院十分别致，你可能会身处其中而不自知，因为其内殿是依岩而建，不施片瓦，却能借崖势遮风避雨，颇具禅趣。

　　语儿泉就在天成禅寺殿堂的右壁，泉水从石隙喷出，水声欢快清脆，好似婴儿牙牙学语。清代书画家沈宗敬有诗《语儿泉》，是此处意境的最好写照："夜半听泉鸣，如与小儿语。语儿儿不知，滴滴皆成雨。"这里的泉水甘冽，若事先备好空瓶，取一些回去冲泡武夷岩茶，细细品鉴，便可知名泉配佳茗之妙处。

　　溪南绝景与九曲风格迥异，却展示着武夷山的另一种美。

Tiger Roaring Rock

Tiger Roaring Rock lying to the north of A Sliver of Sky is the No. I scenic spot in the South Stream area. It got this name because there is a huge hole in the middle of the rock wall and when the mountain winds blow, it sounds like the roar of a tiger, shaking the whole mountain. Tiger Roaring Rock is steep on all sides, stands vertical, and has many natural stones and springs. Eight scenic spots including Tiancheng Zen Temple and Yu'er Spring are distributed on this huge mountain rock. If you want to visit them one by one, you can take the Haohan (Hero) slope pathway that is directly attached to the cliff and is said to be even steeper than Tianyou Peak.

Tiancheng Zen Temple is very exquisite; you may not realize it when you arrive at the temple, because this inner temple is built into the rock, using the rock cliff as its roof.

Yu'er Spring is on the right wall of the temple, and the spring spouts from a stone gap. The gurgling sound is bright and clear, like a baby learning language at an early age. Shen Zongjing, a painter and calligrapher of the Qing Dynasty, wrote a poem called "Yu'er Spring", which is a good portrayal of the fun here. If empty bottles are prepared beforehand, you can take some spring water back to brew Wuyi Rock Tea and taste it carefully; then you may know the magic of the famous spring matched with the famous tea.

The unique scenery of South Stream has a different style from Nine-Bend Stream and displays yet another dimension of the beauty of Mount Wuyi.

◎ 天成禅院的观音浮雕。（郑友裕 摄）
A relief of the Goddess of Mercy at Tiancheng Zen Temple. (Photo by Zheng Youyu.)

◎ 佛国岩下的老建筑。（宋春 摄）
Old buildings under Buddhist Land Rock. (Photo by Song Chun)

■ 佛国岩

　　佛国岩位于武夷山国家级风景名胜区北部，岩体方正，南北向横亘约300米，形似卧佛，人到此处，仿佛置身于佛国之中，膜拜于宝相庄严、端庄肃穆的众佛之下。岩下有佛国寺，现为民居及制茶场所，岩顶、岩麓则有青葱茶园，宁静秀美。这里保留着武夷山国家级风景名胜区唯一一座老茶厂，厂中武夷岩茶传统制作所需要的设备和建筑仍有人在修缮维护，这些年轻一代茶人对于传承的使命感，使他们能够静下心来，坚守于此，书写着自己的故事。

　　出佛国岩，沿茶园北行，便是弥陀岩，与硕大方正的佛国岩相比，它显得纤巧不少，如小尊佛像盘膝坐于蒲团之上。岩麓有弥陀寺，未沾染任何商业气息，里面还存有一块佛教信徒于清道光三年竖立的石碑。弥陀岩也是武夷岩茶名丛的重要场地，山谷之中遍植茶树。弥陀岩、佛国岩虽不如三坑两涧幽深，但是环境和小气候也是出类拔萃的，因为地势相对开阔，日照充足，所产茶叶自有一股劲道十足的霸气。

Foguo (Buddhist Land) Rock

Foguo Rock is located in the north of Wuyishan National Scenic Area. The rock mass is square, about 300 meters long from north to south, and the shape is like a sleeping Buddha. Walking around here feels like going through a Buddhist landscape and worshiping the solemn and pensive Buddhas. Below the rock there is the Foguo Temple. Now however, it is a residential and tea producing area—with green tea plantations on the rock tops and foothills, which are all very serene and beautiful. The only truly old tea factory in Wuyishan National Scenic Area lies here, where the equipment and buildings needed for traditional Wuyi Rock Tea production are still being operated and maintained. It is the sense of mission for their ancient heritage that enables those young tea people to stay here, do things in the old way and create their own stories.

Going out from Foguo Rock, walking north of the tea plantations, you can arrive at Mituo Rock. Compared with the large square Foguo Rock, it appears more slender, like a small Buddha sitting cross-legged on a futon. At the foot of the rock is Mituo Temple, which is free from any commercial activities, and contains a stone tablet erected by Buddhist believers from the Qing Dynasty. Mituo Rock is also an important site of famous Wuyi Rock Tea, and tea trees are planted throughout the valley. Although Mituo Rock and Foguo Rock are not as deep as the Three Pits and Two Ravines, the environment and microclimate are also outstanding because the terrain is relatively open; and with sufficient sunshine, the tea produced here has its own unique taste.

■ 清源岩

清源岩盘峙在山北一块狭窄的谷地上，虽没有令人难忘的风景，却因曾出产过鼎鼎有名的清源茶饼而闻名。清光绪年间，武夷山清源洞住持郑青松得先人秘传，与徒弟倪志元一起制作出能治病的茶饼，且功效显著，畅销一时。郑青松病逝后，倪志元回到家乡泉州，创立倪鸿记茶店，清源茶饼的制作手艺便在倪氏一族中传承，颇受闽南人喜爱，甚至远销菲律宾、新加坡、印度尼西亚等地。1956年，倪志元之子倪郑重将其珍藏的武夷清源茶饼秘传手抄本献给国家，这项古老的技艺在泉州扎下根来，还于2017年被列入了福建省省级非物质文化遗产代表性项目名录。

■ Qingyuan Rock

Qingyuan Rock lies at the bottom of a narrow valley in the North Mountain area. Although there is no memorable scenery, it is still famous because of the Qingyuan Cake-Shaped Tea. During 1875—1908 in the Qing Dynasty, Zheng Qingsong, the abbot of Qingyuan Cave in Mount Wuyi, together with his disciple, Ni Zhiyuan, found a secret recipe of the ancestors and produced cake-shaped tea that could cure diseases. After Zheng died, Ni returned to his hometown in Quanzhou and set up a tea shop. The recipes has been passed down from generation to generation in the Ni family and Qingyuan Cake-Shaped Tea is popular among people in southern Fujian and even exported to the Philippines, Singapore, Indonesia and other countries. In 1956, Ni Zhiyuan's son, Ni Zhengzhong, presented a hand-written copy of the secret recipe to the government. This ancient technique took root in Quanzhou and has been included in the catalogue of Fujian Provincial representative intangible cultural heritage items.

◎ 清源岩。（郑国虎 摄）
Qingyuan Rock. (Photo by Zheng Guohu)

◎ 大地指纹般的茶园。（郑友裕 摄）
A tea plantation looking like fingerprints. (Photo by Zheng Youyu)

■ 妙莲寺

　　妙莲寺深藏于山北莲花峰一处狭长的大型石罅内，为典型的悬空寺，寺体宛若一条长龙盘绕在岩腹，各个内殿均巧妙地建于岩隙之中，无一砖一瓦及任何柱体支撑，彼此之间以石阶和栈道相连，令人叹为观止。栈道栏杆则漆成朱红色，点缀于青山之间，禅意无限，使这里无论是游览还是朝拜，都不失为一个好去处。莲花峰并不高，但是山路曲折，需要一些力气才能登顶。穿过龙形的绝壁栈道，于妙莲寺的回廊处凭栏而立，便可见散落于青山绿水之间的朴素村落及如大地指纹般的茶园。

■ Miaolian Temple

Hidden in a long, narrow rock crack of Lianhua (Lotus) Peak at North Mountain, lies Miaolian Temple, a unique suspended temple, resembling a long dragon coiled in the belly of the rocks. What's amazing is that each inner part of the temple is ingeniously built into the rock gaps without using a brick or a pillar. There are stone steps and plank pathways connecting the parts to each other, and the handrails are painted vermilion. Such a touch of red dotted between the green mountains mirrors the infinite Zen of this place. Miaolian Temple is a good place to go no matter if you are visiting or worshiping. Lianhua Peak is not tall, but it takes some strength to reach the top because of the twists and turns of the mountain path. Through the dragon-shaped cliff plank road, and standing on the cloistered railing of Miaolian Temple, you can see local villages scattered below between the green mountains and blue waters, as well as tea plantations, looking like fingerprints on the earth.

◎ 妙莲寺。（郑友裕 摄）
Miaolian Temple. (Photo by Zheng Youyu)

山北地势平坦，交通便利，是探秘寻幽的好去处。如今，大武夷超级山径赛的线路把溪南和山北都包括其中，使更多人得以领略武夷两极的风采。和一位武夷山本地的参赛者聊天，他说："跑步，已经成为我日子里的一条清晰而生动的脉络，并且和武夷岩茶息息相关。"

武夷岩茶的春茶制茶季特别考验茶人的身体素质，三周的高强度劳动，只靠激情是断然不行的，务必需要一个好身体。"做茶"，其实是和茶青配合完成一次旅行，有点儿像跑步——协调、均衡、专注，并于其中探索自我。

村上春树在《当我谈跑步时我谈些什么》里写道："对我们至关重要的东西，几乎都是肉眼无法看见，然而用心灵可以感受到的。"

在山中行走、跑步，人生变得很丰富。

North Mountain has flat terrain, so it is an easy place to explore. Today, the route of Mount Wuyi Trail Race covers both South of the Stream and North of the Mountains, so more people can enjoy the beauty of the two poles in Wuyi. A local participant said, "Running has become a clear and vivid vein in my life and is closely related to Wuyi Rock Tea."

The spring tea-making season especially tests the physical ability of tea workers. There are three weeks of high-intensity labor. It's impossible to rely only on one's passion. A healthy body is a must. "Making tea" is actually a journey best completed by working with the fresh leaves, much like running an endurance race—coordination, balance, concentration, and pushing oneself to the limit.

Murakami wrote in *What I Talk About When I Talk About Running*, "The things that matter to us (runners) are almost invisible to the naked eye, but they can be felt by the mind."

Walking and running in the mountains makes life very rich and colorful.

◎ 大武夷超级山径赛。（彭善安 摄）
Mount Wuyi Trail Race. (Photo by Peng Shan'an)

罕见的物种基因库——武夷山国家级自然保护区

武夷山国家级自然保护区位于武夷山、建阳、光泽三个县市的结合部，西北部与江西省铅山县比邻，地理坐标为东经117°27′~51′、北纬27°33′~54′，东西最宽处约20千米，南北最长处约54千米，总面积为565.27平方千米。

由于地壳运动，抬升、褶皱、断裂、剥蚀等地质活动曾经在此处频繁发生，从而形成高山、峡谷、孤峰和绝壁等特殊地貌，造就了今日山雄、谷狭、滩险、水秀、季相分明、奇花遍野、芳草铺地、古木参天的优良环境。这里禽兽徜徉、虫鱼自由，是植物的圣地、动物的乐园。

1987年9月，武夷山国家级自然保护区被联合国教科文组织"人与生物圈计划"国际协调理事会接纳为世界生物圈保护区。1999年12月，武夷山被列入世界文化与自然遗产名录，成为双世遗地，自然保护区被列为生物多样性保护区，成为中国仅有的拥有多重世界品牌的自然保护区。

A Rare Species Gene Pool—Wuyishan National Nature Reserve

Wuyishan National Nature Reserve is located at the junction of Wuyishan City, Jianyang County and Guangze County. Northwest it is adjacent to Yanshan County in Jiangxi Province. Its geographical coordinates are 117°27'~51' east longitude and 27°33'~54' north latitude. The widest section is about 20 kilometers from east to west, and the longest is about 54 kilometers from south to north. The total area is 565.27 square kilometers.

As a result of crustal movement, erosion and other geological activities which formed high mountains, narrow valleys, solitary peaks and cliffs and other unique landforms, thereby creating today's wonderful environment here of mountains, vales, shoals, waters, distinct seasons, different kinds of flowers, green grass spreading over the ground, towering ancient trees, etc., Wuyishan National Nature Reserve is also a special paradise for plants and animals.

In September 1987, Wuyishan National Nature Reserve was accepted as a World Biosphere Reserve by the International Coordinating Council of UNESCO's "Man and the Biosphere Program". In December 1999, Mount Wuyi was added to the World Cultural and Natural Heritage List, becoming a double world heritage site, and the nature reserve was listed as a biodiversity reserve, becoming the only nature reserve with such multiple world distinctions in China.

◎ 大竹岚初雪。（郑友裕 摄）

The first snow at Dazhulan. (Photo by Zheng Youyu)

武夷山国家级自然保护区优越的自然条件、丰富的植物种类、完整的森林生态系统、多种多样的生态小环境为野生动物的繁衍提供了理想的栖息地。这里拥有地球同纬度带中面积最大、最典型、保存最为完整的中亚热带原生性森林生态系统；这里是中国小区域单位面积上野生动物资源最为丰富的区域之一，被列为中国陆地生物多样性保护的11个关键地区之一，是世界闻名的生物模式标本产地。

这里的挂墩、大竹岚、三港等地是享誉世界的生物圣地，有着"昆虫世界""蛇的王国""鸟的乐园""研究亚洲两栖爬行动物的钥匙"等美称，是世界公认的生物之窗。

The superior natural conditions, abundant plant species, complete forest ecosystem and diverse microecological environments in Wuyishan National Nature Reserve provide an ideal habitat for wildlife. It has the largest, most typical and most intact subtropical primeval forest ecosystem compared to other places at this same latitude zone on the earth. It is also one of the regions with the richest number of wildlife species per unit area in China. It is listed as one of the eleven key regions for the protection of terrestrial biodiversity in China, and it is a world-famous home of biological type specimens.

Guadun, Dazhulan, San'gang and some other places here provide a world-renowned heaven for wildlife, with the reputation of "insect world", "snake kingdom", "bird paradise", "key to studying Asian amphibians and reptiles", etc., and is recognized as a window into the world's natural life.

◎ 蛇的王国。（郑友裕 摄）
The snake kingdom. (Photo by Zheng Youyu)

在武夷山国家级自然保护区这方动植物的"天然避难所"里，目前已知植物种类有3,728种，可见到鹅掌楸、银杏、南方铁杉、武夷蹄盖蕨等珍稀植物，被列入《中国植物红皮书：稀有濒危植物》的达28种，被冠以"武夷"种加词的就有20多种。目前已知的动物种类有5,110种，其中哺乳纲71种、鸟纲256种、鱼纲40种、两栖纲35种、爬行纲73种、昆虫纲4,635种，被列入国际《濒危野生动植物种国际贸易公约》的动物有46种。此外，武夷山国家级自然保护区还拥有大量稀有特有动物种类，如两栖类的崇安髭蟾、武夷湍蛙等，爬行类的丽棘蜥、挂墩后棱蛇等，鸟类的白眉山鹧鸪、挂墩鸦雀等，哺乳类的猪尾鼠、中华斑蝠等，鱼类的武夷厚唇鱼等。

◎ 武夷山珍稀植物：左为白豆杉，右为鹅掌楸。（文脉 供图）
Rare plants in Mount Wuyi: the pseudotaxus chienii (left) and the tulip tree (right). (Courtesy of Wenmai)

Wuyishan National Nature Reserve is a "natural shelter" for plants and animals, and at the present time, there are 3,728 known plant species. You can see the tulip tree, ginkgo biloba, south hemlock, Wuyi athyrium roth and other rare plants, 28 of which are listed in *Chinese Plant Red Data Book: Rare and Endangered Plants*, and more than 20 species are named with the "Wuyi" specific epithet. At present, there are 5,110 known animal species, including 71 mammals, 256 birds, 40 fishes, 35 amphibians, 73 reptiles and 4,635 insects, 46 of which are listed in *Convention on International Trade in Endangered Species of Wild Fauna and Flora*. In addition, Wuyishan National Nature Reserve also has a large number of rare and unique animal species, such as the amphibious Chongan moustache toad, Wuyi Tuan Frog, the reptile Liji lizard, Guadun Houleng snake and birds like Baimei Mountain Partridge, Guadun crow tit, mammals like pig-tailed rat, Chinese spotted bat, fish like Wuyi thick-lip fish.

◎ 武夷山珍稀动物：左上为崇安髭蟾，右上为藏酋猴，下为黄腹角雉。（郑友裕 摄）
Rare animals in Mount Wuyi: a Chongan moustache toad (upper left), Tibetan macaques (upper right) and a yellow-bellied tragopan (below). (Photo by Zheng Youyu)

早在19世纪40年代，就有外国传教士和生物学家到武夷山采集标本，其中那位被称为"维多利亚时代的邦德"的英国植物学家罗伯特·福琼，将武夷山的茶种和茶苗秘密地带去了印度，使有着5,000多年历史的中国种茶、制茶技术流传到海外，改变了世界茶叶历史。

自19世纪下半叶法国传教士在这里收集到许多动植物新种之后，武夷山引起了西方生物学界的广泛关注。此后有众多的外国博物学者到这里进行生物学考察和收集。美国人后来在三港设立的一个教堂，几乎成为外国收集者的常驻标本采集基地。

世界上许多著名的自然博物馆，如法国国家自然历史博物馆、英国自然历史博物馆、德国柏林自然历史博物馆、美国自然历史博物馆、美国国立博物馆和中国上海自然博物馆都有大批出自武夷山的动物标本，其中有数百种成为模式标本。20世纪前期分别由英国和美国出版的《中国东部的鸟类手册》及《中国的爬行动物》等有影响的著作，都与这一地区有着密切的渊源关系。

As early as in the 1840s, foreign missionaries and biologists came to Mount Wuyi to collect specimens. The "Victorian James Bond" Robert Fortune, a botanist from England, was one of them. He secretly took the tea seeds and tea plants of Mount Wuyi to India, and Chinese tea planting and processing technologies were thus revealed to other countries, which changed the world's tea history.

Ever since French missionaries collected many new species of plants and animals here in the second half of the 19th century, Mount Wuyi had attracted extensive attention from Western biological circles. Since then, a large number of foreign naturalists had come here for biological investigation and collection. The Americans later set up a church in San'gang that became a resident base for foreign collectors.

◎ 武夷山国家级自然保护区正山小种红茶产地。（郑友裕 摄）

The producing area of lapsang souchong black tea in Wuyishan National Nature Reserve. (Photo by Zheng Youyu)

Many famous natural museums in the world, such as those in Paris, London, Berlin, New York, Washington and Shanghai, have a large number of animal specimens from Mount Wuyi, among which hundreds became type specimens. Influential works such as *A Handbook of the Birds of Eastern China* and *The Reptiles of China* respectively published in Britain and the United States in the early 20th century were also closely related to this region.

武夷山被列入世界文化与自然遗产名录后，当地政府出台了科学的保护措施，"保护即发展"的观念越来越深入人心，武夷山国家级自然保护区管理局开始控制大众旅游，开展生态科普教育。当地一些村民受聘成为护林员，接受专业的指导，参与自然区的保护工作，他们学会了与群山为伴，与草木为友，每天往返于崎岖的山路，检测武夷山野生动物的活动情况，搜集自然环境的变化信息，守护自己的绿色家园。

山与水完美结合，人文与自然有机相融，人类与动植物相互依存、活力共生——这样的武夷山是承载天地灵气的遗世杰作，是大自然的一方圣土，是人类的珍稀宝地。

◎ 武夷山国家级自然保护区的科学考察活动。（詹丽英 摄）
The scientific expedition in Wuyishan National Nature Reserve. (Photo by Zhan Liying)

◎ 武夷山国家级自然保护区之夏。（郑友裕 摄）
Wuyishan National Nature Reserve in summer. (Photo by Zheng Youyu)

After Mount Wuyi was added to the World Cultural and Natural Heritage List, the local government introduced scientific protection measures, and the idea that "protection is development" became more and more popular. Wuyishan National Nature Reserve Administration began to control public tourism access and carried out ecological education. Some local villagers were hired as forest rangers to receive professional guidance and participate in the protection of the natural habitat. They have learned to watch over the mountains and make friends with plants and trees. They travel along the rugged mountain roads every day to check the activities of wild animals in Mount Wuyi, collect information about changes in the natural environment and protect the green homeland.

The perfect combination of mountains and water, the organic integration of humanity and nature, and the interdependence and vitality of human beings, animals and plants—Mount Wuyi is a world-renowned masterpiece carrying the essence of the heaven and earth, a sacred land of nature, and a rare treasure for human beings to explore and experience.

沉睡的古越文明——闽越王城遗址

闽越王城遗址坐落在武夷山市兴田镇城村，是中国长江以南保存比较完整的一座汉代古城址。它在选址、建筑手法和风格上独具特色，为当时全国地方诸侯国都邑的代表和典范，体现了业已消逝的闽越古国文明。

据考古研究，该遗址的始建年代最早可能是西汉前期，即闽越国统治时期。闽越国是福建历史上地方割据政权中存在时间最长、也最为强盛的诸侯国。闽越王无诸的先祖为越王勾践的后裔，遭遇灭国之痛后率余部退至福建，与当地先民融合而居。无诸称得上是"开闽始祖"，他立国称王，建立闽越国，揭开了福建文明史的第一页。在将近一个世纪的岁月中，闽越人既保持了福建远古文化中的风俗习惯、宗教信仰等，又在政治、经济、文化、艺术等方面仿效中原内地，创造出灿烂一时的闽越文化。

◎ 闽越王像。（郑友裕 摄）
The statue of King Minyue. (Photo by Zheng Youyu)

The Slumbering Ancient Yue Civilization—Minyue Kingdom Site

Minyue Kingdom Site is located in Chengcun Village, Xingtian Township, Wuyishan City. It is an ancient Han Dynasty city site in relatively good preservation state compared with other ancient Chinese cities unearthed to the south of the Yangtze River. Being unique in site selection, architectural techniques and styles, it was representative of the national capitals of various vassal states at that time, embodying the vanished ancient civilization of Minyue.

According to archaeological research, the earliest construction time of the site was probably in the early Western Han Dynasty, around 202 BC. Minyue was the most powerful vassal state in the history of Fujian Province and existed for the longest time. The founder, Wuzhu, could trace his forbears to the descendants of Emperor Goujian, who led the remainder of their army to retreat to Fujian after suffering the pain of the destruction of their homeland in the north. They settled down and lived with the local people. Wuzhu is called "the ancestor of Fujian" because he proclaimed himself king and established the State of Minyue, opening the first page of the history of Fujian civilization. In less than a century, the Minyue people not only kept the customs and religious faith of the ancient culture of Fujian, but also created a splendid Minyue culture by acclimating much of the central plain's politics, economy, culture and art.

◎ 遗址上的石雕。（郑友裕 摄）
A stone carving at the site. (Photo by Zheng Youyu)

闽越王城遗址占地面积约为48万平方米，建在起伏的丘陵地带上，2,000多米长的夯土城墙轮廓依稀可辨。城墙上建有城楼、烽火台，布局严谨，风格与秦都汉宫相似。两座城门位于城址南部，东西遥望，有直道相通。城内已探明大型建筑群基4处、冶铁作坊遗址5处、居住区15处，以及排水系统、古道路等多处。城内高胡坪是王城的中心建筑区，大型宫殿建筑遗址内有正殿、侧厢、庭院、天井、排水沟等，保存相当完整。遗址自1958年试掘以来，陆续出土了数万件汉代文物，具有很高的价值，其中有许多在全国同类文物中位居前列，如全国最大的花纹空心砖、全国最长的铁矛头、全国最早的顺形陶制下水管道、宫中豪华浴池。这些文物分别代表着当时中国文明的最高水平，一部分就在遗址附近的博物馆展出。

Covering an area of about 480,000 square meters, the ruins of Minyue Kingdom stretches on a hilly land, and the outline of its rammed earth city wall of more than 2,000 meters long is still distinguishable. There are gate towers and beacon towers on a rigorous layout, the style of which is similar to those in the Qin and Han dynasties. The two main gates were located in the south of the city, respectively on the east and west sides—a straight lane directly linking them. In the city, they have discovered 4 large building complex bases, 5 iron mill sites, 15 residential areas, as well as drainage systems, ancient roads and other ruins. Gaohuping is the central building area. The ruins of large palaces contain the main halls, side compartments, courtyards, patios and drainage ditches, which are quite intact. Since the site was tentatively excavated in 1958, thousands of Han Dynasty cultural relics of high value have been unearthed successively, many of which are in the forefront compared to similar cultural relics in the country, such as the largest hollow brick with decorative pattern, the longest iron spearhead, the earliest pottery sewage pipes, and a luxurious bathing pool in the palace. These cultural relics represent the highest level of Chinese civilization at that time and many of them are on display in the museum at the site.

◎ 遗址上出土的陶制下水管道。（郑友裕 摄）
A pottery sewage pipe unearthed. (Photo by Zheng Youyu)

最让游客津津乐道的古城排水系统是利用自然山坡、沟谷建成，雨水、污水分流，规划十分巧妙合理，古人的智慧令人惊叹。大殿北部还有御井一口，至今仍然水质纯净，清洌可饮，被称为"华夏第一古井"，是遗址上唯一还有生命力的旧物。

今天的闽越王城遗址空旷苍凉，那些对历史不感兴趣的人站在此处，或许会觉得意兴阑珊，然而历史就是这样，不断向前，却也默默沉淀，无论你是否为它驻足，古王城都穿越悠悠岁月，静静展示一个古老王国的辉煌往事与厚重文化。

The drainage system of the ancient city, which is the most talked about feature by tourists, is built by using natural slopes and ravines, with rainwater and sewage flowing separately. The design is very clever and well thought out—the wisdom of these ancient people was amazing. There is a royal well in the north of the hall known as "the first ancient well of China", in which the water is still pure, cool and drinkable. Sadly, it is the only vital thing still of use in these ancient ruins.

Today, Minyue Kingdom Site is deserted. People who are not interested in history may feel unimpressed, but time is like this—it keeps going forward; whether or not you want to stop and think about it, the ancient city endures through time, quietly showing an ancient kingdom with a glorious past and rich culture.

◎ 王城御井。（郑友裕 摄）
The royal well. (Photo by Zheng Youyu)

理学之光

The Light of Neo-Confucianism

◎ 朱熹自画像。（郑友裕 摄）
The self-portrait of Zhu Xi. (Photo by Zheng Youyu)

世间名山大川、历史古迹何其多也，能成为世界遗产的却寥寥无几，只有那些具有"突出普遍价值"者才能当选。武夷山能成为世界文化与自然双重遗产，离不开大自然的鬼斧神工赋予这里的独特之美，也少不了朱熹及朱子理学带给它的文化内涵。

宋代著名理学家朱熹，是孔孟之后中国历史上最伟大的思想家、哲学家和教育家，是儒学思想的后期代表人物。朱熹承前启后，开创新儒学——朱子理学，被钦定为官方的正统哲学思想，成为南宋至清代700多年间一直处于统治地位的思想理论，影响着中国社会生活的各个方面，并且漂洋过海，传播范围远及东亚、东南亚及欧美一些国家。

"宇宙间三十六名山，地未有如武夷之胜；孔孟后千五百余载，道未有如文公之尊。"武夷山作为朱子理学的摇篮，曾经汇集了中国最有才华的一批人，故而熠熠生光，是自古以来无数人想要寻幽探胜的地方。

Few of the world's most famous mountains, rivers and historical sites are world heritage sites. Only those with "outstanding universal values" can be selected. Mount Wuyi became a dual world heritage site not only due to its unique beauty carved by nature's celestial workmanship, but also for the special cultural aspects infused into the natural beauty by the great philosopher Zhu Xi and Neo-Confucianism.

Zhu Xi, a famous Song Dynasty Confucian scholar and the foremost representative of the late stage of Confucianism, was the greatest thinker, philosopher and educator in Chinese history after Confucius and Mencius. Zhu Xi promulgated the rebirth of Confucianism, which was officially recognized as the official philosophical thought, and had been the dominant ideology from the Southern Song Dynasty to the Qing Dynasty—a period of more than 700 years! It influenced all aspects of Chinese social life and spread far across the sea, as far as East Asia, Southeast Asia and some European and American countries.

"Of the 36 famous mountains in the universe, there is no other special mountain like Mount Wuyi; more than 1,500 years after Confucius and Mencius, there is no one so honorable as Zhu Xi." Mount Wuyi, as the cradle of Zhuzi's Neo-Confucianism ("Zhuzi" is another honorific name of Zhu Xi meaning "Master Zhu"), once hosted a group of the most talented scholars in China—so shining was this place in ancient times that countless people journeyed here to relax, explore and learn.

From the translator: About Mount Wuyi Zhu Xi once wrote, "I once heard the elders say that central Fujian was a paradise. I spent my first years in the (Wuyi) mountains only, ignorant of what happened outside them. After I arrived (in Zhejiang) I knew why my hometown was indeed a paradise."

But before we get into "Neo-Confucianism" maybe we should update a little on Confucianism. Confucius lived, wrote and taught almost 1,500 years before Zhu Xi. And during that long period of history, many of his works were lost, destroyed or devoured by worms. He did, however, teach over 3,000 disciples who themselves taught even more and it was these disciples and their descendants who kept Confucianism alive throughout the years. But everything, even great teachings, tend to get stale after 1,500 years. And during that time there were other philosophies and movements which rose and fell in popularity (Buddhism, Taoism, and others). So by the Song Dynasty, the country was ripe for a spring cleaning of philosophy.

◎ 朱子理学摇篮——武夷山。（郑友裕 摄）

The cradle of Zhuzi's Neo-Confucianism—Mount Wuyi. (Photo by Zheng Youyu)

道南理窟

武夷山的晚对峰上有一处引人注目的摩崖石刻——"道南理窟"，这四个苍郁古雅的擘窠大字概括了武夷山的理学渊源。

"理窟"意即武夷山乃理学荟萃之宝地。

"道南"之说来自于北宋理学奠基人程颢。当年，程颢的得意门徒杨时、游酢学成南归福建，他在家乡河南颍川送别弟子时说："吾道南矣！"自此，理学南传，杨时、游酢后来于武夷山讲学、著述，终老于斯。

游酢在武夷山五曲筑水云寮，著《易说》《诗二南义》，广收学生，传道授业，渐渐使他的学术理论得以完善与推广。他传播理学的主要功绩在于将程颢平时的言行记录整理成书，作《明道先生语录》，成为开闽学先河者，被尊称为"道南儒宗"。

The Southern Neo-Confucianism Grotto

In the Wandui Peak area of Mount Wuyi, there is a striking cliff stone inscription—"Dao Nan Li Ku (The southern Neo-Confucianism grotto)". These four strong and quaint characters announce to the world that Neo-Confucianism origins at Mount Wuyi.

"Li Ku" means that Mount Wuyi is a treasured place for Neo-Confucianism.

"Dao Nan" originated from Cheng Hao, founder of Neo-Confucianism in the Northern Song Dynasty. When Cheng Hao's favorite disciples Yang Shi and You Zuo completed their study and went back south to Fujian, he said to them in his hometown in Yingchuan of Henan, "My theory spreads to the south!" Since then, Neo-Confucianism spread to the south of China. Later Yang Shi and You Zuo gave lectures, wrote books and passed away in Mount Wuyi.

You Zuo built Shuiyun Hut at the fifth bend and wrote books. He also gathered around him many disciples, and his teachings gradually improved and promoted his academic theories. The main achievement of Neo-Confucianism by You Zuo was to compile Cheng Hao's daily speeches and teachings into a book, *Quotations from Mr Mingdao*. You Zuo thus became the pioneer of Fujian Confucian studies and was honored as the "ancestor of Confucianism in southern China".

◎ "道南理窟" 摩崖石刻。（郑友裕 摄）
The cliff inscription "The southern Neo-Confucianism grotto". (Photo by Zheng Youyu)

理学一派自此在武夷山一带植根繁衍，历南宋、元、明、清数代，经久不衰。历史上著名的理学家接踵而来，藏修著述，学成而归，传播硕果。胡安国、胡宏，"东南三贤"朱熹、吕祖谦、张栻以及蔡元定、蔡沈、黄幹、刘火仑、真德秀、魏了翁等名儒前后相继，传播理学。特别是深受游酢理学思想影响、理学集大成者朱熹，在武夷山生活达50年之久，与其师友门徒在理学研究上堪称一枝独秀，形成闽学。

元仁宗年间，朝廷下诏，将武夷山学者胡安国的《春秋传》、朱熹的《四书章句集注》《诗集传》、蔡沈的《书集传》列为科举取士的经文定本，从此武夷山在学术上长期处于全国领先的地位。

《崇安县新志》对此不无自豪地写道："自此，本邑学术执全国之牛耳而笼罩百代矣！"

著名历史学家蔡尚思进而寓论于诗："东周出孔丘，南宋有朱熹。中国古文化，泰山与武夷！"

◎《四书章句集注》。（郑友裕 摄）
Variorum for the Four Books. (Photo by Zheng Youyu)

The Neo-Confucianism school became rooted and flourished in the Mount Wuyi area, lasting from the Southern Song, and through the Yuan, Ming and Qing dynasties. Many famous scholars in history came one after another, writing books, teaching and then returning to their hometowns after they finished their studies, spreading their knowledge. Zhu Xi, who was deeply influenced by You Zuo's thoughts of Neo-Confucianism and became a master himself, lived in Mount Wuyi for 50 years. Together with his teachers, friends and disciples, he outshone other scholars in the study of Neo-Confucianism and formed the Min (Fujian) Studies.

During 1312—1320 in the Yuan Dynasty, the imperial court issued an imperial edict that listed the works of Mount Wuyi scholars, Hu Anguo's *Notes to Spring and Autumn Annals*, Zhu Xi's *Variorum for the Four Books*, *A Study on the Book of Songs*, and Cai Shen's *Notes to the Book of History* as the standard text of the imperial examination. Since then, Mount Wuyi had been in a leading position in the philosophic academic field.

The New County Annals of Chongan wrote proudly that, "Since then, our county gained leadership of the whole country's academia and their study influenced a hundred generations!"

Cai Shangsi, a famous historian, wrote in his poem, "The Eastern Zhou Dynasty had Confucius and the Southern Song Dynasty had Zhu Xi. Mount Tai and Mount Wuyi nourished ancient Chinese culture!"

◎ 《诗集传》。（郑友裕 摄）
A Study on the Book of Songs. (Photo by Zheng Youyu)

从朱熹到朱子

朱熹（1130—1200），字元晦，后改仲晦，别号晦庵，晚年自称晦翁、云谷老人、沧州病叟、遁翁等，祖籍南宋徽州婺源（今江西省婺源县）。朱熹于南宋建炎四年出生于福建尤溪，14岁丧父后，随母定居于崇安五夫里（今武夷山市五夫镇），卒于宁宗庆元六年，终年71岁。朱熹死后，朱宁宗谥曰"文"，世称朱文公，理宗时被追封为"信国公"，从祀孔庙，是唯一非孔子亲传弟子而能享祀孔庙之人，被后世尊称为"朱子"。

朱熹的一生与武夷山有着十分密切的关系。800多年前，14岁的朱熹跟随母亲来到武夷山，按照父亲的临终嘱咐投靠其生前好友。从这以后，他除了"仕宦九载，立朝四十六天"外，半个世纪都是在武夷山度过。

武夷山与朱熹相关的遗迹很多。据文献记载，武夷山朱熹讲学处有武夷精舍、冲佑观、水帘洞、金谷洞四处，朱熹手书的石刻有10余处。朱熹赞颂武夷山的诗文甚多，其中尤以淳熙十一年（1184）所作的《九曲棹歌》最为精彩。这首棹歌对九曲溪各曲特色风景的描绘有如神来之笔，显示了朱熹对于武夷山水的熟悉与热爱，之后作诗应和此歌者众，故有"棹歌首唱自朱熹"之说。

From Zhu Xi to Zhuzi

Zhu Xi (1130—1200), whose ancestral home was at Wuyuan, Huizhou (now Wuyuan County, Jiangxi Province) was born in Youxi, Sanming, Fujian Province in the fourth year of Jianyan in the Southern Song Dynasty. At the age of 14, his father died; Zhu Xi and his mother then settled in Wufuli, Chongan (now Wufu Town, Wuyishan City). After the death of Zhu Xi, Song Dynasty Emperor Ningzong honoured him the posthumous title of "Wen" and Emperor Lizong honoured him "Duke Xinguo". He was the only person who was not an actual disciple of Confucius but entered the Confucius Temple and was enshrined. He was later honored as "Zhuzi"—Master Zhu.

Zhu Xi's whole life had a close relationship with Mount Wuyi. More than 800 years ago, Zhu Xi, who was 14 years old, followed his father's dying wish and moved with his mother to Mount Wuyi where his father's friend lived. From then on, he spent half a century in Mount Wuyi except for "nine years of official service and 46 days of going to court".

There are many historical mementos related to Zhu Xi in Mount Wuyi. According to the records, Zhu Xi gave lectures in several places in Mount Wuyi, including Wuyi Academy, Chongyou Taoist Temple, Water Curtain Cave and Jingu Cave, and there were more than 10 stone inscriptions of Zhu Xi's calligraphy. Zhu Xi wrote many poems to praise Mount Wuyi, among which the most splendid one is the *Nine-Bend Rowing Song*, written in 1184. This song depicts the unique scenery of each bend of Nine-Bend Stream in a display of literary and visual genius, which exemplified Zhu Xi's love for Mount Wuyi. After that, there were a lot of people who wrote poems in response to this song, so it is said that "The rowing song was first sung by Zhu Xi."

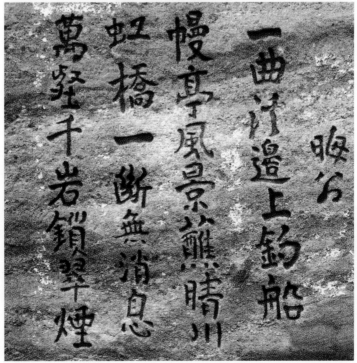

◎ 朱熹手书石刻。（郑友裕 摄）

Stone inscriptions of Zhu Xi's calligraphy. (Photo by Zheng Youyu)

山，静止承载，慷慨给予；水，随机应变，恩泽万物。或许正是武夷山的青山绿水，启发了朱熹的无尽才思，他的学说"致广大、尽精微、综罗百代"，成为南宋以来时代精神的表征，中国传统文化的主流。"家孔孟而户程朱"，反映了朱熹理学对中国人的深刻影响。

朱熹的一生，是学术研究与著书立说相伴的一生。朱熹著有《周易本义》《易学启蒙》《诗集传》《楚辞集注》《韩文考异》《家礼》《仪礼经传通解》《资治通鉴纲目》《四书章句集注》等。他思考人在宇宙中的地位、探索政治哲学、寻找精神修养之法，成就了一个博大宏伟的思想体系，中国古代执政者从中寻求治国理政的哲学，老百姓从中获得安身立命的智慧，读书人从中总结修身济世的信条。

朱熹特别注重讲学立道，创立修葺书院20多所，门生达几千人。他亲自制定书院学规，把《四书章句集注》作为教材，这种学习形式至元明已成为书院通行的教育方法。朱熹认为，书院的教育宗旨是教学生博学、审问、慎思、明辨、笃行，另外还要修身、处事、践行，而非空泛读书。

因理学家的推动与实践，南宋民间书院空前繁荣，朱熹则是推动书院发展的最得力者，这些既有独立品格、又有学术品质的书院，可以说是中国大学最早的雏形。

◎ 考亭书院（朱熹晚年讲学处）遗址。（郑友裕 摄）
The site of Kaoting Academy, where Zhu Xi lectured in his old age. (Photo by Zheng Youyu)

The mountain, majestic form and strength; the water, pliable function and strength. Perhaps it was the green mountains and clear waters of Mount Wuyi that inspired Zhu Xi's endless creative thought. His theory of "To achieve a broad macro state (form), at the same time go deep into the micro details (function), and to synthesize the wisdom of every generation" has become the symbol of the Chinese spirit since the Southern Song Dynasty, as well as a mainstay of traditional Chinese culture. Zhu Xi's Neo-Confucianism had a profound and lasting influence on the Chinese people and culture.

Zhu Xi devoted his life to doing academic research, teaching and writing. His works include *The Original Meaning of I-Ching, The Enlightenment of I-Ching Learning, A Study on the Book of Songs, Variorum for the Songs of Chu, Proofreading of Works About Han Yu, Family Etiquette, A General Explanation of the Books of Rites and Other Books About Etiquette, The Synopsis of the Comprehensive Mirror for Aid in Government, Variorum for the Four Books*, etc. He thought about man's position in the cosmos, explored political philosophy, and sought for the ways of spiritual cultivation, which made a broad and magnificent ideological system, from which ancient Chinese rulers sought wisdom for governing the country, ordinary people gained the practical guidance for establishing oneself, and scholars gained the guidance for cultivating one's morality, wisdom, benevolence and virtue.

Zhu Xi paid special attention to both learning and teaching. He founded more than 20 academies and gathered thousands of students. He made the rules of these academies by himself and used *Variorum for the Four Books* as the basic teaching material, which developed into a general method of education during the Yuan and Ming dynasties. According to Zhu Xi, the educational purpose of an academy was to teach students not to just read, but rather to learn, interrogate (e.g. learn by questioning), think carefully, distinguish clearly and practice earnestly.

With the promotion and practice of Neo-Confucianism scholars, the academies in the Southern Song Dynasty flourished. Zhu Xi was the most prominent and effective scholar to promote the development of academies. These academies with independent characteristics and high academic standards can be said to be the earliest form of universities in China.

朱子认识论可以归结为"格物致知"四字。"格，至也，物，犹事也。穷至事物之理，欲其极处无不到也。"用现代语言解释，或许就是穷究事物道理，致使智慧、心得感悟与知识通达至极。

朱子本人对"格物致知"身体力行，上至天文地理，下到飞鸟走兽，他都细细探究。他曾自制浑天仪，观测星象。他比西方天文学家开普勒早四五百年发现了雪花为六边形的事实。朱熹对《周易》研究的成果，特别是在其所撰《周易本义》中对伏羲八卦方位图、伏羲六十四卦方位图（后演变为阴阳回互相抱的古太极图）的解释，极大地影响了西方学者莱布尼茨和波尔，引发了现代物理大师探索和创造的灵感。波尔曾公开表示，他的量子理论的互补概念同东方古典文化的太极阴阳思想有惊人的一致。莱布尼茨则受此启发发明了二进位制，于是有了电子计算机。莱布尼茨说："人们说二进位制是我的首创，准确地说应该是朱熹。"

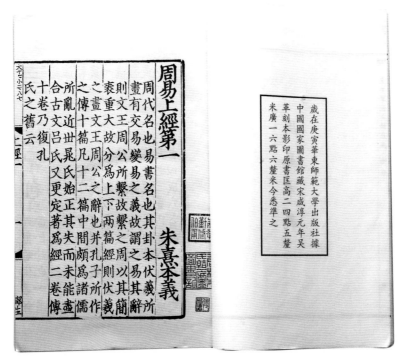

◎《周易本义》。（郑友裕 摄）

The Original Meaning of I-Ching. (Photo by Zheng Youyu)

Zhuzi's epistemology can be summed up by the words "Learning by experience". It means to learn through contact with things, experientially by doing, not just theoretical thinking. We can truly understand the "natural principles" of things by moving from the superficial to the subtle, from the whole to the part, and from the phenomenon to the essence behind it, step by step.

Zhu Xi practiced this himself, from astronomy and geography, to birds and animals. He explored them all carefully. He made his own telescope and observed the stars. He discovered the hexagonal shape of snowflakes four or five hundred years before the western astronomer Kepler. Zhu Xi's research on *The Book of Changes,* especially his explanation on Fu Hsi 8 and 64 hexagrams positional charts (later evolved into the ancient Taiji diagram of Yin and Yang embracing each other) in *The Original Meaning of I-Ching,* greatly influenced Leibniz and Bohr, the great masters of modern physics, and inspired their investigations and inventions. Bohr once publicly stated that the complementary concept of his quantum theory is strikingly consistent with the idea of Taiji Yin-Yang in oriental classical culture. Leibniz was inspired to invent the binary system, which led to the invention of the electronic computer. Leibniz said, "People say I was the first person to invent the binary system. Actually, it should be Zhu Xi."

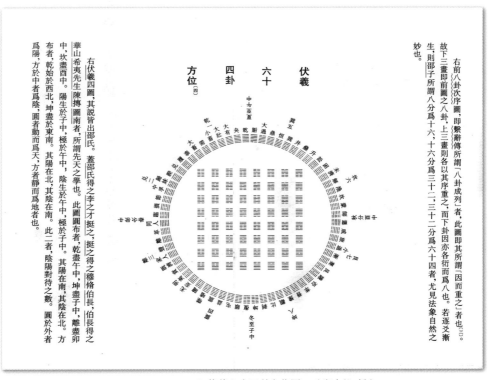

◎ 伏羲六十四卦方位图。（郑友裕 摄）

The Fu Hsi 64 hexagrams positional chart. (Photo by Zheng Youyu)

莱布尼茨在1715年写下《致德雷蒙先生的信：论中国哲学》，表达他直到暮年仍然尊崇和向往中国理学家那种思想开放、独立思考、富于思辨的品格和崇尚理性的信念。《中国科学技术史》作者李约瑟则说："当爱因斯坦时代到来时，人们发现一长串的哲学思想家已经为之准备好了道路——从怀特海上溯到恩格斯和黑格尔，又从黑格尔到莱布尼茨——那时候的灵感也许就完全不是欧洲的了。也许，最现代化的欧洲的自然科学理论基础应该归功于庄周、周敦颐和朱熹等人的，要比世人至今所认识到的更多。""至少理学的世界观和自然科学的观点极其一致。""宋代理学本质上是科学性的。"

"格物穷理"与西方近代实证科学精神竟有如此神交，令人感慨。

著名学者钱穆先生高度评价了朱熹在中国理学史上的地位。他说："在中国历史上，前古有孔子，近古有朱子。此两人皆在中国学术思想史及中国文化史上发出莫大声光，留下莫大影响。旷观全史，恐无第三人堪与伦比。"

或许，是时候重新认识朱熹了。

In 1715 Leibniz wrote *A Letter to Nikolai Remon on Chinese Philosophy*, expressing his respect and yearning until his old age for Chinese Neo-Confucianists' open-mindedness, independent thinking, speculative character and rational belief. Joseph Needham, the author of *Science and Civilisation in China*, said, "When the Einstein era came along, people 'discovered' a long line of philosophical thinkers that had already prepared the way for it—from Whitehead to Engels and Hegel to Leibniz—but the inspiration might not have been from Europe at all. Perhaps the most modern European theories of the natural science owe more to Zhuang Zhou, Zhou Dunyi and Zhuzi than the world has ever realized or acknowledged." "At least the worldview of Neo-Confucianism is extremely consistent with that of the natural science." "Neo-Confucianism in the Song Dynasty was scientific in nature."

It is amazing that Zhu Xi's admonition, "experience things to get the essence", has the same basis as modern empirical science in the west.

Qian Mu, a famous scholar from Taiwan, spoke highly of Zhu Xi's position in the history of Chinese Neo-Confucianism. He said, "In Chinese history, there was Confucius in ancient times and Zhuzi in the nearest antiquity. Both of them have made a great impact on the history of Chinese academic ideology and Chinese culture. Look at the whole history, and you will find that no one is comparable."

Maybe it's time to "rediscover" Zhu Xi.

◎ 朱熹雕像。（郑友裕 摄）
The statue of Zhu Xi. (Photo by Zheng Youyu)

武夷三翁

钱穆先生还曾感慨说："朱子倘不入道学儒林，亦当在文苑传中占一席地，大贤能事，固是无所不用其极也。"

朱熹和著名的诗人陆游、词人辛弃疾是同时代人。三人在武夷山有过交集，被尊称为"武夷三翁"（陆放翁、辛瓢翁、朱晦翁）。后人对这段三星聚首于道南理窟的辉煌历史向来津津乐道。

在讲他们之间的故事之前，有必要先讲讲冲佑观。

武夷冲佑观故址位于今武夷宫范围内，它是武夷山最古老的一座宫观，迄今已有1,200多年的历史。冲佑观始创于盛唐天宝年间，当时称天宝殿。唐玄宗曾派大臣来武夷山，封其为"名山大川"，并立有碑记。至唐末，闽王王审之大兴土木，进行扩建，天宝殿改名为武夷观。南唐时皇帝李璟为他的弟弟李良佐入观修道而重修殿宇，并将其改名为会仙观。北宋年间殿宇增修，改称冲佑观，并由宋真宗赐观额，成为宋代六大名观之一。

Three Sages in Wuyi

Qian Mu also said with deep emotion, "Even if Zhuzi had not mastered Taoism and Confucianism, he would also occupy a great place in the field of literature. Great and wise men can do everything with all their might."

Zhu Xi was a contemporary writer with the famous poets, Lu You and Xin Qiji. The three crossed paths in Mount Wuyi and were honored as the "Three Sages in Wuyi". Posterity relishes this glorious history of three great poets gathering in Mount Wuyi, the grotto of Confucianism.

Before telling the story about them, it is necessary to talk about Chongyou Temple.

The former site of Wuyi Chongyou Temple was located within the grounds of today's Wuyi Palace. It is the oldest palace in Mount Wuyi with a history of more than 1,200 years. Chongyou Temple was founded in the Tang Dynasty, then known as Tianbao Palace. Emperor Xuanzong once sent his ministers to Mount Wuyi, and named it "A famous mountain with great rivers". At the end of the Tang Dynasty, Wang Shenzhi, the president of Fujian reconstructed and expanded this structure, and renamed it Wuyi Temple. In the Southern Tang Dynasty, Emperor Lijing rebuilt the temple for his younger brother, Li Liangzuo, to practice in, and renamed it as the Huixian Temple. During the Northern Song Dynasty, the temple was renovated and renamed Chongyou Temple, and a plaque was presented by Emperor Zhenzong. Later it became one of the six famous temples in the Song Dynasty.

© 冲佑观旧址，今武夷春秋馆。（郑友裕 摄）
Wuyi Spring and Autumn Hall, the former site of Chongyou Temple. (Photo by Zheng Youyu)

冲佑观规制有如公署，按照宋代朝廷的官制，祠禄之官分为提举、提点、管勾（即主管）、和监，共四级，用以安置一些闲官冗员和与朝廷政见不合之人。

冲佑观曾为宋代理学家的驻足之处。朱熹、叶适、吕祖谦、魏了翁、张栻、彭龟年等人都曾任冲佑观主管或提举，因此，这个著名的道教宫观在宋明理学的发展史上占有重要的地位。

淳熙二年（1175）起，朱熹受命主管冲佑观长达四年，这期间，他完成了《论语集注》和《孟子集注》这两部中国哲学史上的重要著作。除此之外，他还写就《家礼》，后来成为指导家庭伦理纲常的手册。朱熹在这本书中设计并系统化的家礼可以应用于人生的各个阶段，成为士大夫阶层的行为规范。加拿大汉学家卜正民认为，《家礼》让朱熹在朝鲜和日本也享有巨大声誉。

◎ 纪念朱子诞生880周年国际座谈会。（郑友裕 供图）

An international colloquia to commemorate the 880th birthday anniversary of Zhuzi. (Courtesy of Zheng Youyu)

Chongyou Temple served as an "official" temple and had certain rules and regulations. According to the Song Dynasty official system, there were four officials assigned to the temple with different ranks who enjoyed stipends, including Tiju, Tidian, Guangou (the director), and Hejian (the inspector). It was, in reality, a place to settle idle officials and dissidents.

In the Song Dynasty, Chongyou Temple became a home for Neo-Confucianists. Zhu Xi and some other famous scholars were former supervisors there. Therefore, this famous Taoist temple occupies an important position in the history of the development of Neo-Confucianism.

In the second year of Chunxi (1175), Zhu Xi was appointed to be in charge of Chongyou Temple for four years. During this period, he completed two important works in the history of Chinese philosophy, *Variorum for the Analects of Confucius* and *Variorum for the Book of Mencius*. In addition, he wrote *The Family Etiquette*, which later became a handbook of family ethics. In this book, Zhu Xi compiled and systematized family rituals that could be applied to all stages of life and became the code of conduct for the scholar-official class. According to Bu Zhengmin, a Canadian sinologist, Zhu Xi also enjoyed a great reputation in Korea and Japan because of this handbook.

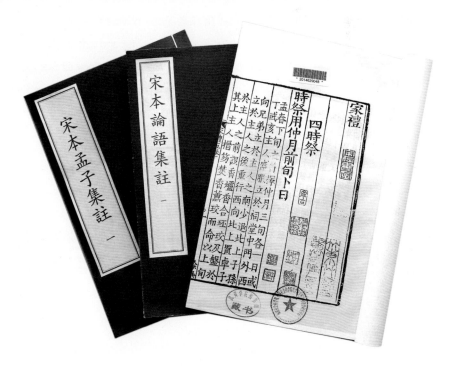

◎ 《家礼》内页。（郑友裕 摄）

An inside page of *The Family Etiquette*. (Photo by Zheng Youyu)

武夷三翁中的陆放翁陆游是著名的爱国诗人，曾前后两次任冲佑观提举。淳熙初年，陆游慕名游览武夷山，与朱熹初识于山中。二人都热爱文学，且同怀忧国忧民之思，常有书来信往，纵情谈论，情深意切。

陆游被贬回绍兴后，朱熹曾托人辗转千里，送上武夷纸被，陆游为此赋诗："纸被围身度雪天，白于狐腋软于绵。"朱熹还曾以武夷茶作为礼品馈送陆游，陆游写下《喜得建茶》一诗回谢。陆游年届花甲时被贬官，赋闲家中，听闻朱熹在武夷山兴修的武夷精舍竣工，遥寄贺诗四首，以"未读晦翁新著书"表达挚友之心。

庆元四年（1198），朱熹涉祸文字狱，被列为党禁的罪魁之一，两年后殁于建阳，陆游闻讯，挥泪写下祭文："捐百世起九原之思，倾长河注东海之泪。路修齿耄，神往形留。公殁不忘，庶其歆飨！"

Lu You, one of the Three Sages in Wuyi, was a famous patriotic poet who was assigned to be Tiju of Chongyou Temple twice. In the early years of Chunxi, Lu You visited Mount Wuyi and met Zhu Xi there in the mountains. Both of them loved literature and shared a deep concern for the country and the people. They often sent letters to each other, talked without reserve, and became very close friends.

Later Lu You was banished to Shaoxing, so Zhu Xi sent someone to travel thousands of miles to give him a warm Mount Wuyi quilt (a quilt made of vine fiber). Lu You wrote a poem, "Wrapped in the quilt on a snowy day, it is white as fox fur and soft as silk." Zhu Xi also sent the Wuyi tea as a gift to Lu You, and he replied with a poem *Happy to Get the Tea* to thank him. When Lu You was near his 60th year, he was again demoted and stayed idle at home. When he heard that Zhu Xi's Wuyi Academy had been completed, he sent four poems of congratulation to express his best friend's glad heart.

In 1198 Zhu Xi was involved in a literary inquisition and listed as one of the offenders banned by the government. Two years later in 1200, he died in Jianyang. Hearing the news, Lu You wrote a heartfelt elegy with tears, "I would rather die a hundred times instead of you. My tears flow to the east sea like the rushing water of the river. The road is so far and I am old. Although I can't see you again, my heart will always follow you. Even you have left us, but you always live in people's hearts."

From the translator: Confucius also suffered many setbacks and frustrations in his own life, but he once said, "The orchid growing in a distant mountain meadow does not stop giving off its fragrance even though there is no one there to enjoy it. Neither will a man of virtue and benevolence abandon his cause because of setbacks."

The fragrance and essence of the teachings of Confucius and Zhuzi continues to bring enjoyment to millions of people even today.

◎ 宋代爱国诗人陆游画像。（壹图网 供图）
A portrait of Lu You, the famous Song Dynasty patriotic poet. (Courtesy of www.1tu.com.)

武夷三翁中的辛弃疾因长期寓居江西铅山县的瓢泉，被尊称为"瓢翁"。辛弃疾先后三次被贬到武夷山冲佑观任祠官，其间常与结庐山中的朱熹议政论义，酬唱应对，彼此引为知己。理学家陈亮称他们一个是"人中之龙"，一个是"文中之虎"，堪称南宋的"双子星座"。

公元1193年8月的一天，朱熹和辛弃疾在九曲溪上进行了武夷山人文历史中著名的观光之旅。与好友同游，泛舟九曲，朱熹唱出脍炙人口的《武夷棹歌》，而辛弃疾亦作棹歌十首相和。当夜，朱熹又为辛弃疾的二斋室写下"克己复礼"与"夙兴夜寐"的墨宝。

辛弃疾曾作《酬朱晦翁》，诗曰："历数唐尧千载下，如公仅有两三人。"

朱熹病逝，辛弃疾在《祭朱晦庵文》中感叹："所不朽者，垂万世名。孰谓公死，凛凛犹生！"

在辛弃疾心中，朱熹是屹立在滚滚洪流中的砥柱山。

日本学者村上哲见评价他们之间真挚的友谊时说："一个善于思考的人与一个敢作敢为的人能结交厚谊，令人钦佩，令人深思。"

The third sage, Xin Qiji, was honored as "Piao Weng " because he lived at the Piao Spring of Yanshan County in Jiangxi Province for a long time. Xin Qiji was banished three times to Wuyi Chongyou Temple, during which time he often discussed politics and justice with Zhu Xi, and they became close confidants of each other. Chen Liang, a Neo-Confucianist, called them "the dragon among men" and "the tiger in literature" and the "Gemini constellation" of the Southern Song Dynasty.

One day in August 1193, Zhu Xi and Xin Qiji made a famous sightseeing trip down Nine-Bend Stream. Travelling with friends, boating up the nine bends, Zhu Xi sang the popular *Nine-Bend Rowing Song*, and Xin Qiji also composed 10 rowing songs in response to him. That night, Zhu Xi wrote two pieces of precious calligraphy works "Discipline yourself so that everything is ritual" and "Get up early and go to bed late to be a diligent man" for Xin Qiji's Erzhai Study.

Xin Qiji once wrote a poem for Zhu Xi, "In the thousands of years of history after Yao and Shun, there are only two or three people like you."

When Zhu Xi died, Xin Qiji sighed in his elegy, "Those who are immortal are forever remembered. You die as if you were alive!"

In Xin Qiji's heart, Zhu Xi was like a mountain pillar standing erect through the rolling torrent of history.

Japanese scholar Murakami Zhejian wrote of their sincere friendship, "It is admirable and thought-provoking that a thoughtful person and an aggressive person can make friends."

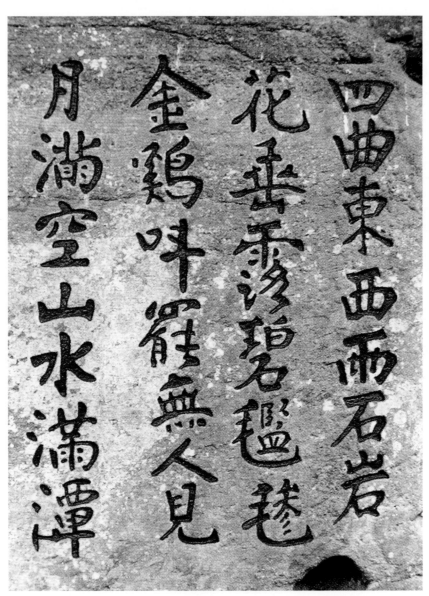

◎《武夷棹歌》之四曲。（郑友裕 摄）
The rowing song for the fourth bend. (Photo by Zheng Youyu)

理学朝圣

朱熹随母定居于五夫里（现为五夫镇）之后，从学于父亲的生前好友刘子翚及胡宪、刘勉之三位先贤，在五夫的屏山书院，勤学苦读，17岁中举，19岁中进士，脱颖而出。朱熹居于五夫紫阳楼40多年，五夫，是他的另一个故乡。

一个人居住和生活的环境会影响他的思考方式，也会影响他对周遭的看法。在五夫镇慢慢踱步，处处可见朱子的影子，不由会想到那个"仁"字，果实里柔软的内核——生生也。

睹物思贤，不妨来趟理学朝圣之旅。

A Pilgrimage to Neo-Confucianism

After settling down in Wufuli (now Wufu Township) with his mother, Zhu Xi studied hard at Pingshan Academy in Wufu under the guidance of his father's former friends Liu Zihui, Hu Xian and Liu Mianzhi. Zhu Xi lived in Ziyang Building for more than 40 years. Wufu is considered his second hometown.

The environment in which a person lives can greatly affect the way he thinks and the way he views his surroundings. From a slow pace in Wufu Township, you can see the steady footprints of Zhuzi, and remember his views on "benevolence".

Why not make a pilgrimage to Wufu Township to experience firsthand the birthplace of Neo-Confucianism?

◎ 五夫镇朱子雕像。（郑友裕 摄）

The statue of Zhuzi at Wufu Township. (Photo by Zheng Youyu)

■ 朱子巷

民间俗称朱始巷。它是五夫里五夫街的一条叉巷，始建于五代十国的南唐时期，至今已有1,000多年的历史。朱子巷原长300米，现仅存138米，巷子口立有"朱子巷"石碑，路面由鹅卵石铺就，两侧皆是古屋高墙，行走其中，古趣盎然。朱熹居于五夫里的那些年，无论是幼时谒师，还是成年后求学访友、外出论道，每次出门都要走过这条小巷。后人为纪念这位理学的集大成者，便将这条小巷称为朱子巷。著名的美籍华裔学者陈荣捷瞻仰朱子故居时至此巷，曾亲自丈量古巷宽度，并向海外学者介绍说，宏博如海洋的朱子学诞生于如此狭小的陋巷中，恰是朴素辩证法"泰山不弃细石，江河不拒涓流"的一个佐证。

■ *Zhuzi Lane*

People also call it Zhushi Alley. It is a branch lane off Wufu Street, first built during the Southern Tang Dynasty, with a history of more than 1,000 years. Originally 300 meters long, there is only 138 meters left now. At the entrance of the alley, there is a stone monument engraved with "Zhuzi Lane". The pavement is paved with cobble stones. During those years when Zhu Xi lived there, he set off from this lane every time he went out, whether as a youth when he went to study with his teachers or as an adult to visit friends and be out to experience life himself. Later generations called it Zhuzi Lane to commemorate him, as the one who most epitomized Neo-Confucianism. When Wing-tsit Chan, a famous Chinese American scholar, paid his respect to Zhuzi's

◎ 朱子巷。（郑友裕 摄）
Zhuzi Lane. (Photo by Zheng Youyu)

former residence in this lane, he measured the width of the ancient lane in person, and expounded to overseas scholars that although Zhuzi's school of philosophy and knowledge was as broad as the ocean, it was born in this narrow and nondescript lane, which is similar to the idiom that "Mount Tai does not abandon small rocks and big rivers do not refuse mere trickles".

■ 兴贤古街

　　兴贤古街是五夫镇的一条古老街道，始自五虹桥，终至文献桥（又名双龙桥），由籍溪坊、中和坊、儒林坊、朱至坊、紫阳坊、双溪坊六个街坊组成，全长1,000余米，以朱子过化之胜而闻名。

　　兴贤古街牌坊林立，可见多处历史名人手书横额，"天地钟秀""崇东首善""籍溪胜境""紫阳流风""三峰鼎峙""三市街""过化处""天南道国""邹鲁渊源"等等，吸引着你去一一探究背后的渊源历史、人文掌故。街坊两侧矗立着兴贤书院、刘氏家祠、连氏节孝坊等古迹，韵味悠远。

　　南宋后期，朱熹、胡家五贤、刘家诸贤相继成名后，兴贤古街已是名人学者云集。从中晚唐时期初具雏形，至宋代鼎盛，1,000余年的世故沧桑，值得细细品味。

◎ 兴贤古街一角。（郑友裕 摄）
A corner of Xingxian Ancient Street. (Photo by Zheng Youyu)

Xingxian Ancient Street

Xingxian Ancient Street is an old street in Wufu Town, which starts from Wuhong Bridge and ends up in Wenxian Bridge (also known as Shuanglong Bridge). It is composed of six neighborhoods; the total length is more than 1,000 meters, and it is also famous because of Zhuzi.

There are numerous memorial archways in Xingxian Ancient Street, where you can see many handwritten banners by famous historical figures, which entices you to learn more about the history, culture and anecdotes behind them. On both sides of the neighborhood stand Xingxian Academy, Liu Clan Ancestral Hall, Lianshi Chastity and Filial Piety Memorial Archway and other historical sites, with lingering charm and cultural significance.

In the late Southern Song Dynasty, after Zhu Xi and other sages in the Hu and Liu families became famous successively, Xingxian Ancient Street was always full of famous scholars. From the middle and late Tang Dynasty to the peak of the Song Dynasty, showing more than 1,000 years of the flow of Chinese philosophical thought—it is truly a place worthy to linger and savor the historical significance.

◎ 连氏节孝坊。（郑友裕 摄）
Lianshi Chastity and Filial Piety Memorial Archway. (Photo by Zheng Youyu)

◎ 兴贤书院。（郑友裕 摄）

Xingxian Academy. (Photo by Zheng Youyu)

■ 兴贤书院

　　兴贤书院位于五夫镇兴贤古街，始建于南宋孝宗（1163—1189）年间，是为纪念理学先贤胡宪而兴建。

　　书院牌楼飞檐层叠，气势夺人，石砖上雕有花鸟人物，栩栩如生，彰显着昔日此处的地位与荣光。全部建筑共分三进，处处庄重典雅。前进为正堂，分下廊与上厅，下廊设有两厢房；二进为书院，分左右两院；三进为文昌阁。书院门楼屋檐顶上供奉着"状元""榜眼""探花"三顶官帽，至今仍然清晰可见，这便是古代读书人的最高追求了。可以想见，古时曾有多少学子，伫立此处，举目端详，或立下志向，或暗自兴叹。

　　朱熹学有所成后，曾在该书院讲学授徒。

■ Xingxian Academy

Xingxian Academy, located in Xingxian Ancient Street, was built during 1163—1189 in the Southern Song Dynasty in honour of Hu Xian, an ancient Neo-Confucian scholar.

The upturned eaves of the academy archway are stacked in an imposing manner with lifelike flowers and birds carved on the stone bricks, showing the former imperial status and favor here. The building is divided into three parts, and everywhere it is solemn and elegant. The first part is the main hall which is divided into the lower hall and the upper hall—the lower hall had two side rooms. The second part is the academy, divided into two yards, and the third part is Wenchang Pavilion. On the eaves over the gateway of the academy, three official caps of "Zhuangyuan", "Bangyan" and "Tanhua" (representing the top three applicants who scored the highest during the ancient imperial examinations) are enshrined, and which are still clearly visible today. These were the ancient scholars' highest pursuit. We can imagine how many students once stood there in ancient times, looking up at the three caps, either making ambitious promises to themselves or praying for themselves.

After Zhu Xi realized his high achievements, he taught in this academy.

◎ 书院屋顶的状元帽。（郑友裕 摄）
Zhuangyuan's cap on the eave. (Photo by Zheng Youyu)

书院的外墙上有一种精美的砖雕图案，为龙头鱼身，当地人称之为"鱼化龙"。这是流传于民间的吉祥形象，暗示着学子们只要潜心苦读，就可鱼跃龙门，变成天之骄子。五夫民间至今仍保留着有千年历史的龙鱼戏表演。表演者用竹子扎成鱼龙形骨架，裹上绢布，绘上色彩，制成龙鱼灯，另外还要制作牙旗灯、水纹灯、龙门灯，与锣鼓队、唢呐队、燃放队配合进行表演。传说从宋代起，每逢士子中举登榜时，乡邻便以此庆祝。如今，每年正月十五，当地村民也会自发组织表演队，走街串巷进行表演，祈求年年有余，吉祥如意。

◎ "鱼化龙"砖雕。（郑友裕 摄）
The "fish becomes the dragon" pattern. (Photo by Zheng Youyu)

On the outer wall of the academy, there is an exquisite brick carving pattern, which has a dragon head and a fish body, known locally as the "fish becomes the dragon". This is an auspicious image in the folk lore, suggesting that as long as students dedicate themselves to hard study, they can jump over the dragon gate and become "God's favoured ones" (treasured fish). Wufu folks have retained the dragon fish imagery through a thousand years of cultural performances. The performers tie bamboo into a fish-dragon skeleton, wrap it in silk cloth and paint colors to make dragon/fish lanterns. In addition, they make Yaqi lanterns, water-pattern lanterns and dragon gate lanterns and accompany them with gong and drum teams, suona horn teams and fireworks teams. It is said that since the Song Dynasty, when local scholars' names were released on the official examination list, their neighbors would celebrate. Today, on the fifteenth day of the first lunar month, villagers here also organize such teams to perform street to street to celebrate and pray for abundance and good luck for the year.

© 龙鱼戏表演。（郑友裕 摄）
The dragon-fish performance. (Photo by Zheng Youyu)

◎ 朱子社仓。（宋春 摄）
Zhuzi Charitable Granary. (Photo by Song Chun)

■ 朱子社仓

　　朱子社仓坐落在五夫里籍溪坊（今五夫镇兴贤街）之凤凰巷内，是朱熹为赈济灾民于南宋乾道七年（1171）所创建，因社仓地址在五夫里，又名"五夫社仓"。

　　社仓在青黄不接时以低利贷粮，百姓收成后于冬季偿清本息，有灾赈灾，无灾济贫，大利于民，被后人誉为"先儒经济盛迹"。一时间，各地纷纷效仿。邑人为了纪念先贤朱熹的这项惠民善政，改称"五夫社仓"为"朱子社仓"。

Zhuzi Charitable Granary

Zhuzi Charitable Granary is located in Fenghuang (Phoenix) Lane of Wufuli Jixi Neighborhood (now Xingxian Street in Wufu Township), which was founded by Zhu Xi to relieve the victims of famine or adversity during the Southern Song Dynasty in 1171. Because the storehouse is in Wufuli, it is also known as "Wufu Granary".

People could borrow grain at a low interest rate when their old grain had been exhausted before the new crops became ripe for harvesting, and paid off the principal and interest later in winter. The granary was also used for disaster relief, or if there was no disaster, it served as poverty relief, which was of great benefit to the local people and known as the "Confucian economic assistance". After Zhu Xi established this system in Wufuli, other places followed suit one after another. In order to commemorate Zhu Xi's good governance, the granary was renamed "Zhuzi Charitable Granary".

◎ 社仓正门。（郑友裕 摄）

The front door of the granary. (Photo by Zheng Youyu)

■ 紫阳楼

　　紫阳楼为朱熹故居，位于五夫镇屏山脚下，潭溪之畔。由朱熹昔日诗文可知，这里曾经是一座五间开的房子，门前辟有菜地、鱼塘，周围可栽树种花。朱熹从14岁开始在这里读书、思考，成名后也在此讲学、授徒、著述，使紫阳楼成为朱子理学萌芽、成熟和向外传播的地方。

　　古时紫阳楼前就有着成片的莲田，历史上曾有"闽邦渊源水清清，朱子故里荷田田"的记载。如今，诗中情景依旧在，千年荷塘依然春华秋实，种莲、收莲蓬、剥莲子，延续千年的传统营生在乡人朴实的日子里传承。

　　每年六七月间，数不清的荷花亭亭玉立于碧波之上，引人驻足，五夫观荷已成旅游新风向，待到莲子上市，则又添美食。五夫白莲曾是唐、宋、清时期的宫廷贡品，是这片山水的慷慨馈赠。朱子故里的特色名吃五夫莲子炖蛋洁白无瑕，入口即化，莲香与蛋香相得益彰。在武夷山全茶宴中，高厨还会尝试用位列五大名丛的白鸡冠为这道菜添上茶味，着实妙不可言。

■ **Ziyang Building**

Ziyang Building is Zhu Xi's former residence, located at the foot of Ping Mountain in Wufu Town, beside Tan Stream. According to Zhu Xi's poems, there was once a five-room house with vegetable fields and a fishpond

n front of it, and trees and flowers were planted around it. Zhu Xi began to read and study here at the age of 14. After becoming famous, he also taught, lectured and wrote here, making Ziyang Building a place where Zhuzi's Neo-Confucianism germinated, matured and started its endless journey throughout the world.

There have been lotus fields in front of Ziyang Building since ancient times. According to a poem, "At the birthplace of the Min school, the water is clear; in the hometown of Zhuzi, the lotus fields are green." Today, the scene is still like the poem. There are still blossoms in summer and fruits in autumn in the millennium-old lotus fields. Lotus planting, harvesting, seeds peeling—villagers continue the long tradition of livelihood and the simple way of life.

Every year in June and July, countless lotus blossoms rise on the green water ripples, attracting people to stop and enjoy the scene. Viewing Wufu lotus has become a new trend of tourism. When the lotus seeds ripen, Wufu Town becomes a good place to enjoy delicious food. As a popular gift from this landscape, the Wufu white lotus seed was also once an imperial tribute of the Tang, Song and Qing dynasties. The famous local dish, Wufu Lotus Seeds Stewed in Egg Custard, is immaculately white, melting in your mouth while the fragrance of lotus and egg complement each other. At the Wuyishan tea banquet, senior chefs also try to add tea flavor to the dish with Baijiguan, one of the five most famous teas in Mount Wuyi—it is delicious beyond description.

◎ 五夫荷田。（郑友裕 摄）
The lotus field at Wufu Township. (Photo by Zheng Youyu)

◎ 紫阳楼旧址。（郑友裕 摄）

The former site of Ziyang Building. (Photo by Zheng Youyu)

　　紫阳楼还有神道碑、灵泉和朱子手植古樟，流连其中，引人遐思。恩师刘子翚为朱熹取字"元晦"，并在朱熹16岁时为他举行成人仪式，要求他亲手种下这棵樟树，取《易经》中的"木晦于根，春容晔敷；人晦于身，神明内腴"，喻义处事做人必须首重修身，如同树木繁茂首先在于根。朱熹在65岁时曾写下对联："佩韦遵考训，晦木谨师传"，表示自己一生遵循父亲的亭训和恩师的教诲。如今斯人已逝，800多岁的古樟却依然亭亭如盖，就像朱子理学，无论世事如何变迁，抑或经受多少误解，其中精华，依然给后人以启发和滋养。

Around Ziyang Building, there are also the Divine Monument, Ling Spring and an ancient camphor tree planted by Zhu Xi, which stimulates people's imagination. Zhu Xi's mentor, Liu Zihui, chose Yuanhui for Zhu Xi as a courtesy name and held an adulthood ceremony for him when he was 16 years old and asked him to plant the camphor tree by himself. The implication was that one must first cultivate his morality; just as a tree grows through its roots, man grows through his morality. Zhu Xi wrote a couplet when he was 65 to show that he had obeyed this edification his whole life. Zhu Xi has passed away, but the ancient camphor, which is more than 800 years old, still flourishes gracefully, just like Zhuzi's Neo-Confucianism thought—no matter how the world changes or how much misunderstanding there is, the essence of it still enlightens and nourishes posterity.

◎ 朱子手植樟。（郑友裕 摄）
The camphor tree planted by Zhuzi. (Photo by Zheng Youyu)

From the translator: An afterthought—very few people throughout all recorded time have had such a transformational effect on hundreds of millions of people's lives continuously over a period of 700 years and which continues even today. Buddha, Laozi, Jesus, Confucius, Zhu Xi ... the list is short.

As I mentioned previously, he unified the three religions of Oriental thought (Buddhism, Taoism and Confucianism). Then he codified his research into readable texts using the new printing and papermaking technology. His works touched not just philosophy but also literature, history, music and the natural sciences.

To Zhu Xi the supreme being of the universe was Taiji, i.e. the original source of the world and myriad things. (The Taoists called it the Tao, the Way.) From this came the Yın/ Yang and then everything else followed. The Taiji was like space, boundless, eternal, absolute, and perfect—no inside/ outside, no up/ down, no right/ left. The problem finding it is that it is non-physical, i.e. you cannot find it using your physical senses—it is a no-thing (Wu-Ji), the non-ultimate—so you must use other means; that is what is hinted at by his words, "seeing but not seeing", "hearing but not hearing".

Buddhism which became very popular throughout China advocated two ways to get there (i.e. to get the "other shore"; to find the Supreme being). The first one was reciting and studying the sutras painstakingly over many years and hopefully you would receive enlightenment; the second way could be much quicker—instantaneous self-realization (Chan & Zen Buddhists) which was triggered by a sudden awakening of the Truth (which was inside you all the time), but even then it was usually preceded by many years of study.

Zhu Xi, like Confucius, sought after this same Truth in a similar manner, i.e. the first manner, getting there gradually (Jian-Jin) through learning knowledge and by investigating things to understand their true essence. These two great men never stopped reading, pondering and learning during their entire lives. Do you remember that inscription from section 4, "Gradually entering the beautiful scenery"?

The second way propounded by Zhu Xi was quicker, almost instantaneous—a sudden enlightenment (Dun-Wu). This is similar to the Chan/ Zen enlightenment—one day it just comes to you, the key; it's so simple and it's been there right before your eyes all the time.

Zhu Xi took umbrage at others' methods, e.g. the Chan/ Zen method of using the koans (those senseless riddles)—once Zhu Xi said to a disciple, "They show the embroidered ducks to others; yet do not show the gold embroidering needle." Unfortunately, they couldn't because those gold needles (keys) are different for every person.

One last personal thought about these two great men, Confucius and Zhu Xi: after you get to the other shore (i.e. enlightenment), then what? You can stay there, or you can come back to help others cross (as Buddha and the arhats did). I think these two scholars chose to come back, not so much to enlighten others spiritually but rather to help their beloved country, to teach and encourage scholars and officials to learn many aspects of life, knowledge, benevolence, virtue, etc., and with this knowledge to help humanity prosper. They were philosophers and scholars but underneath it all, patriots.

风物之赞

Ode to Wuyi Specialties

◎ 武夷岩茶核心产区之一——倒水坑。（郑友裕 摄）
One of the core tea production areas of Mount Wuyi—Daoshui Pit. (Photo by Zheng Youyu)

武夷茶史话

武夷茶最早见诸文字的记载，是唐朝元和（806—820）年间文学家孙樵的《送茶与焦刑部书》："晚甘侯十五人，遣侍斋阁。此徒皆请雷而摘，拜水而和。盖建阳丹山碧水之乡，月涧云龛之品，慎勿贱用之！"其中的"晚甘侯"即指武夷茶。

武夷之茶，兴于唐，盛于宋。唐贞元初年，建茶（武夷山建溪流域所产之茶）发展很快，茶园成片种植，并开始出现规模化制茶。至五代十国时期，建安（今建瓯）富绅张廷晖将其在凤凰山的茶园全部献给闽王，作为皇家茶园，因凤凰山在闽国五都之北，所产之茶称"北苑茶"，这便是北苑御茶园的由来。北苑贡茶由此崛起，朝野瞩目，可谓朝霞初放。

北宋初期，朝廷接管了北苑御茶园，设"官焙"，造龙凤茶，也就是饼状的蒸青团茶。北苑龙凤茶"采摘之精，制作之工，品第之胜，烹点之妙，莫不咸造其极"，誉满天下，成为皇室的心头好。天子除了自己享用之外，也会按照等级分赐给臣僚，以示恩泽。

◎ 今日凤凰山。（吴震 摄）
Today's Fenghuang Mountain. (Photo by Wu Zhen)

The History of Legendary Wuyi Tea

The earliest record of Wuyi Tea can be found in a letter written by the Tang Dynasty litterateur Sun Qiao when he presented tea as gift to an official, which said "I'm sending you Wanganhou for a taste. This tea grows between the red mountains and jade waters of Jianyang (Now Wuyi), picked when the sky thunders, and steamed by the heavenly mists, so the tea is saintly enough to be used for sacrifice. Do not waste." The word Wanganhou in the letter referred to Wuyi Tea.

Wuyi Tea thrived during the Tang Dynasty and reached its peak during the Song Dynasty. In the early years of the Tang Dynasty, Jian tea (produced in the Jian Stream area in Mount Wuyi) developed so fast that many tea plantations and large-scale plantations appeared. During the period of Five Dynasties and Ten Kingdoms, a rich squire named Zhang Tinghui in Jian'an (now Jian'ou County), consecrated his tea plantation in Fenghuang (Phoenix) Mountain to the Min (Fujian) King as a royal tea plantation. Because Fenghuang Mountain lies in the north of Min Kingdom (now Fujian Province), the tea produced there was called Beiyuan (North Garden) Tea, which was well-known to every household.

Later in the early years of the Northern Song Dynasty, the central government took over this royal tea plantation, and began to officially make a tea called Longfeng (Dragon and Phoenix) Tea—the old-style steamed green tea produced in the shape of cakes. Since the tea leaves were selectively picked, skillfully made and artfully roasted, Beiyuan Longfeng Tea reached the peak of perfection. And its name spread throughout the whole country and became the favorite of the royal family. Sometimes, the tea was often gifted to officials and important people by the emperors as a sign of imperial favor.

◎ 黄岗山主峰。（郑友裕 摄）

The main peak of Mount Huanggang. (Photo by Zheng Youyu)

建溪发源于武夷山脉的黄岗山，当时建溪两岸的武夷山、凤凰山、壑源山等处均茶树遍布，所产之茶统称建茶，有"建溪官茶天下绝"之誉。宋朝南渡以后，武夷山渐成理学名山。著名学者荟萃山中，斗茶品茗，以茶促文，以文论道，极一时之盛。而儒、释、道三教汇聚的武夷山，又成为僧道竞相建寺造观的场所，他们凭借武夷茶参禅悟道、修身炼丹，此外亲自种茶，并精研制茶技艺，茶事遂大兴。《崇安县新志》有文曰："宋时范仲淹、欧阳修、梅尧臣、苏轼、蔡襄、丁谓等从而张之，武夷茶遂驰名天下。"

元大德六年（1302），武夷山九曲溪的四曲溪畔创设御茶园，沿袭宋朝制作"龙团凤饼"的工艺，采武夷岩茶焙制龙团，武夷茶脱颖而出，独步入贡。

四曲、五曲、六曲附近是茶园集中的地方，也是优质茶叶的产地，宋、元、明的文字记载中都可以找到有关接笋峰、平林渡、小九曲等地植茶之盛、产品之佳的资料。

Jian Stream originates at Huanggang Mountain, and along the stream there is Mount Wuyi, Fenghuang Mountain and Heyuan Mountain, where a lot of tea trees grow, and the tea produced there was called Jian Tea, proclaiming the fame of "Jian Stream official tea, the best tea in the world". After the central government of the Southern Song Dynasty moved south, Mount Wuyi gradually became a famous mountain of Confucianism, Buddhism and Taoism, and celebrities from all walks of life came here, enjoying the tea ceremonies, the beautiful scenery and the literary environment. They set up temples and monasteries and pursued the spirit of their philosophies, during which the tea served as a good companion. The scholars also planted tea trees themselves and studied tea-making techniques, which was one of the main causes for the Wuyi Tea boom. *The New County Annals of Chongan* said that Fan Zhongyan, Ouyang Xiu, Mei Yaochen, Su Shi, Cai Xiang and Ding Wei, some of the greatest poets and scholars of the time, all enjoyed Wuyi Tea, and this made Wuyi tea well-known to the world.

In 1302, the royal tea plantation was set up at the fourth bend of Nine-Bend Stream in Mount Wuyi. There they followed the technique of making the "Cake-Shaped Tea with a Dragon and Phoenix Pattern". This further made Wuyi tea stand out from other teas as a unique tribute.

Near the fourth, fifth and sixth bends lie additional tea plantations, which also produce tea of excellent quality. From the written records of the Song, Yuan and Ming dynasties, we can find information about the flourishing tea plantations and the excellent products from such places as Jiesun Peak, Pinglin Ferry and Xiao Jiuqu.

◎ 四曲御茶园。（郑友裕 摄）
The royal tea plantation at the fourth bend. (Photo by Zheng Youyu)

◎ 御茶园通仙井。（郑友裕 摄）
Tongxian Well at the royal tea plantation. (Photo by Zheng Youyu)

　　武夷茶入贡给武夷山的茶农带来深重的灾难，茶政扰民，茶农纷纷逃亡，终致"本山茶枯"。明洪武二十四年（1391），朱元璋诏令改芽茶入贡，龙团凤饼制作工艺被炒青散茶工艺所替代。御茶园从此荒废，只留下了一口水味清甜的通仙井。

　　免除上供后的武夷茶农从各级官吏的盘剥中解脱出来，种茶积极性得以恢复，武夷茶的产量和质量又有提升。明隆庆年间，武夷茶人改进工艺，制出介于红茶与绿茶之间的乌龙茶（即现在所称的武夷岩茶），正山小种脱颖而出，也成为世界红茶的鼻祖，武夷茶开始饮誉世界。

　　明永乐年间，郑和下西洋时携带了大量的茶叶作为馈赠礼品，其中就包括武夷茶，自此打开了茶叶外销之门。明万历年间，荷兰东印度公司从澳门收购武夷茶，经印尼爪哇销往欧洲，第一批武夷茶在欧洲亮相即压倒群荗，很快占领了欧洲茶叶市场，欧洲人因此称中国茶为"武夷茶"。瑞典权威植物学家林耐在《植物种志》一书中，以武夷变种（Var Bohea）作为中国小叶种茶树的代表，可见当时武夷茶在世界上的知名程度。

Paying Wuyi tea as tribute was a heavy burden for the tea farmers, and the tea administration was also a nuisance for them, so many fled in succession, resulting in a decline in production; "the tea trees withered on the hills". In 1391, Emperor Zhu Yuanzhang decreed a change in the style of tea tribute, and afterwards the "Cake-Shaped Tea with a Dragon and Phoenix Pattern" producing technology was replaced by stirred loose tea technology. After that time, the royal tea plantation was abandoned, leaving only the sweet water in Tongxian Well.

The tea farmers in Wuyi were freed from exploitation by officials at all levels after the exemption of Wuyi tea, and their enthusiasm for tea planting was restored, and the yield and quality of Wuyi tea improved. During 1567—1572 in the Ming Dynasty, Wuyi tea producers improved their techniques to produce oolong tea (now known as Wuyi Rock Tea, which is between black tea and green tea). Lapsang Souchong stood out and became the ancestor of black tea. Subsequently, Wuyi tea started to enjoy an excellent reputation worldwide.

During 1403—1424 of the Ming Dynasty, Zheng He carried a large amount of tea, including Wuyi tea, as gifts for foreign rulers when he sailed to the West, which helped open the door for Chinese tea exports. During 1573—1619 in the Ming Dynasty, the Dutch East India Company acquired Wuyi tea from Macao and sold it to Europe via Java, Indonesia. The first batch of Wuyi tea overwhelmed the tea drinkers in Europe and soon took over the European tea market. Thereafter, Europeans called Chinese tea "Wuyi tea". Linnaeus, an authoritative Swedish botanist, in his book *Species Plantarum*, took the Wuyi variety (Var Bohea) as the representative of Chinese small-leaf tea trees, which shows how famous Wuyi tea was in the world at that time.

◎ 乌龙茶茶汤。（郑友裕 摄）
The soup of oolong tea. (Photo by Zheng Youyu)

◎ 邹氏家祠。（郑友裕 摄）

The Zou Family's Ancestral Hall. (Photo by Zheng Youyu)

  武夷山下梅村位于武夷山市东部，因地处梅溪下游而得名，距武夷山国家级风景名胜区8千米，是武夷山世界文化遗产地的组成部分。当溪，由西向东穿村而过，将下梅村分为南北两面，使其具备了水运条件。明末清初，下梅发展成为闽北地区最大的茶叶集散地。据《崇安县志》记载："其时武夷茶市集崇安下梅，盛时每日竹筏三百艘，转运不绝。"可窥见当时武夷茶市外运的繁忙景象。

  清代中后期，虽然与武夷山远隔万水千山，却极具商业嗅觉的山西榆次常氏商人与下梅邹氏景隆号茶商联合，从下梅收购茶叶，先运到县城，再用马车载到江西河口登船，然后一路北上，到达中俄边境后，将茶叶转手给恰克图的俄罗斯商人。这条由下梅通往恰克图的茶叶贸易之路，史称"茶叶丝绸之路"，它南起福建武夷山，途经江西、湖南、湖北、河南、山西、河北、内蒙古等地，穿越蒙古国，最终抵达俄罗斯圣彼得堡，全程近两万千米。这条贸易通道，在促进当时的国际经济、文化、宗教交流，推动沿线城市带的兴起与发展等方面起到了重要的作用。

Xiamei Village in the east of Wuyishan City is located in the lower reaches of Meixi River, hence the name. The village is 8 kilometers from Wuyishan National Scenic Area and was inscribed as part of the Mount Wuyi world cultural heritage. Dangxi River flows through Xiamei Village from east to west, dividing it into north and south sides, which was ideal for water transportation. At the end of the Ming Dynasty and the beginning of the Qing Dynasty, Xiamei Village became the largest tea distribution center in northern Fujian Province. According to *The County Annals of Chongan*, "300 bamboo rafts came and went in an endless stream to transport tea every day when Xiamei Village was at its peak."

In the mid and late Qing Dynasty, although not very close to Mount Wuyi, the Chang Family businessmen from Yuci, Shanxi Province realized the commercial value of Wuyi tea, and formed a business partnership with the Zou Family, tea merchants in Xiamei. They bought tea at Xiamei, carried them first through water way to the county, and then took the carriage to the river mouth of Jiangxi. There Wuyi tea travelled north by canal until the Kiakhta merchants took over at the border between China and Russia. This 20 thousand kilometers' long tea trade road, which history calls the "Tea Silk Road" started from Mount Wuyi in Fujian and went via Jiangxi, Hunan, Hubei, Henan, Shanxi, Hebei, Inner Mongolia, etc., all the way to St. Petersburg in Russia. It played an important role in the economic, cultural and religious exchange at that time and in promoting the emergence and development of the urban belt along this road.

◎ 夕阳下的下梅古街。（郑友裕 摄）
The ancient street at Xiamei Village bathing in the sunset. (Photo by Zheng Youyu)

下梅是万里茶路的起点，也是中国历史文化名村和一处中国传统村落。村落依山傍水择址肇基而建的"三街、四埠、五坊、七巷、九堂"格局保存完整，绕祠而筑的闽北特色古民居建筑群沿梅溪、当溪呈串珠状散布于山间盆地，"溪—村"景观独具特色，是闽北地区传统山水村落的典型样本；村内建筑遗产类型丰富，祠堂、书院、寺庙、商铺、别业、码头等沿水系和传统街巷集中分布，砖雕、石雕、木雕精美华贵，所构筑的"古埠茶市"见证过"万里茶路第一站"当年商贾云集、茶市兴盛的昔日辉煌。其中邹家祠堂矗立溪北，依然气势恢宏。今日，这个山环水抱、延续千年的古村落依然静谧安宁美好，是研究武夷茶文化和中外茶叶贸易史的重要基地。

鸦片战争之后，武夷茶开始大量从福州、厦门两个海岸出口。随着时代的更迭，武夷茶的产区也悄然发生转移，自九曲溪逐渐移至三坑两涧。

◎ 下梅木雕。（郑友裕 摄）
Xiamei wood carvings. (Photo by Zheng Youyu)

◎ 下梅砖雕。（郑友裕 摄）
Xiamei brick carvings. (Photo by Zheng Youyu)

◎ 下梅石雕。（宋春 摄）
Xiamei stone carvings. (Photo by Song Chun)

As the starting point of this ten-thousand-mile tea road, Xiamei is a famous historical and cultural village, as well as a traditional Chinese village. Situated at the foot of a hill and beside a stream, Xiamei Village is exquisitely designed and well preserved, with the northern Fujian style ancient dwellings built around the ancestral hall and scattered along Meixi River and Dangxi River like a string of beads in the intermountain basin. This unique "stream—village" landscape is a typical sample of waterside villages in northern Fujian. The cultural heritage in Xiamei is characterized by rich varieties of buildings like ancestral halls, academies, temples, stores, villas and wharfs which mainly concentrate along the stream and alleys and constitute the ancient "tea market by the wharf". The exquisite brick, stone and wood carvings on these buildings witnessed Xiamei's past glory as a place for gathering merchants and flourishing trade. The ancestral hall of Zou Family still stands to the north of the stream today, solemn and magnificent.

After the Opium War, Wuyi tea began to be exported from Fuzhou and Xiamen. With the change of times, Wuyi tea production areas also quietly shifted from Nine-Bend Stream to Three-Pit and Two-Ravine area.

◎ 村中的外国游客。（严家蔚 摄）
Foreign visitors in Xiamei Village. (Photo by Yan Jiawei)

◎ 下梅村婆婆门，相传由邹氏设计，用来衡量未来儿媳妇人选的身材。（郑友裕 摄）
Door of Mother-in-Law in Xiamei Village, designed by Madam Zou to test if the future daughter-in-law is good-shaped.
(Photo by Zheng Youyu)

武夷茶得天独厚的优势

　　武夷山素有"奇秀甲于东南"之美誉。这里群峰相连，峡谷纵横，山水缠绕，气候温润，雨量充沛。武夷岩茶富于岩韵的优秀品质正是源自武夷山碧水丹山的独特自然环境的孕育，有着"臻山川精英秀气所钟"之赞誉。

◎ 山水缠绕的武夷山。（郑友裕 摄）

Mount Wuyi—a picture of mountain and water intertwining. (Photo by Zheng Youyu)

The Unique Advantage of Wuyi Tea

Mount Wuyi has long been known as "the most beautiful scenery in the southeast of China". Mount Wuyi area presents groups of peaks, ravines, streams, all with a warm climate and abundant rainfall. Wuyi Rock Tea is rich in quality due to the unique natural environment of Wuyi mountains. It has been praised as "a delicate collection of mountains and waters".

武夷山西北面群峰耸立，海拔较高，山为屏障，可阻挡北部寒流的侵袭，山谷之中冬暖夏凉，茶树生长于此，可免于冻害、风害。境内有九曲溪、崇阳溪、梅溪、黄柏溪环绕于山峰、沟谷和丘陵之间，山间常年云雾弥漫，有自己独特的微域气候——年平均气温为18.5℃，无霜期长，年降雨量在2,000毫米左右，年平均相对湿度为80%左右，正是茶树喜爱的自然阴湿环境。

被尊为"茶圣"的唐代人陆羽在他所撰写的世界上第一部茶叶专著《茶经》里讲道："其地，上者生烂石，中者生砾壤，下者生黄土。" 武夷山为丹霞地貌，茶园土壤含细碎石或风化石，疏松而透气，大部分茶园土质介于烂石与砾壤之间，对茶树的生长十分理想。

武夷山的茶园主要分布在海拔500米以下的丘陵、低山或沟谷、岩壑之间，日照时间较短，漫射光多，是"佳茗自天成"的好场所。好的山场，亦是一种"共生图谱"的典范。生物的多元共生，直接体现着彼此间关系的"真"。

◎ 云雾弥漫的武夷山。（朱庆福 摄）
The mist-shrouded Mount Wuyi. (Photo by Zhu Qingfu)

From the translator: Let me explain. The soils are made up of crushed ancient rocks, gravel and topsoil—all of which receive their moisture from rains and mists which flow over, under and through these rocks, which are rich in various minerals infusing the tea leaves with a unique taste—called Rock Tea.

Mount Wuyi stands to the northwest of the other peaks acting as a barrier to prevent the invasion of cold northern air currents, keeping the valley warm in winter and cool in summer; likewise the tea trees are protected from freezing and cold winds. There are several streams throughout the area, e.g. Nine-Bend Stream, Chongyang Stream, Mei Stream, Huangbai Stream—flowing around and between the mountains, valleys and hills. The clouds and mists diffuse all year round, creating a micro domain with its own unique micro-climate—annual average temperature is 18.5°C, with a long frost-free period, and about 2,000mm annual rainfall (annual average relative humidity is 80%); so, it is a perfect natural moist eco-environment for tea trees.

Tang Dynasty Lu Yu, who is revered as the "saint of tea", said in *The Classic of Tea*, the world's first tea treatise: "For growing tea, the soil with broken stones is best, the gravel soil is moderate, and the loess soil is inferior." Mount Wuyi is a Danxia landform (layered sandstones) and the soil of the tea plantations contains fine gravel or weathered granite, which is loose and breathable. Most of the soil is in a state between broken stones and gravel soil, which is very ideal for the growth of tea trees as it allows for good root drainage.

Tea plantations in Wuyi mountains are mainly distributed in the hills and low mountains not higher than 500 meters above sea level, or ravines and rock gullies. With a short sunshine time and diffused light, these are excellent places where "good tea grows from heaven". Good mountain fields are also a model of a "symbiosis map". The multiple symbiosis of organisms directly reflects the "truth" of the relationship between them.

◎ 白鸡冠。（郑友裕 摄）
White Cockscomb. (Photo by Zheng Youyu)

　　武夷山素有"茶树品种王国"之称。历代茶人潜心探索，从菜茶（"天产"野生茶种）中选育出多种茶树名丛。由宋至明，再到清末的武夷岩茶全盛时期，武夷山孕育了"四大名丛"——铁罗汉（宋）、白鸡冠（明）、大红袍（清中叶）和水金龟（民国初年），此外还有半天腰、不知春、金锁匙、白瑞香、白牡丹、水仙、肉桂等珍贵品种。

　　武夷山独特的盆栽式茶园也与其他茶区不同。武夷山茶区地形错综复杂，大部分山场是利用幽谷、深坑、岩隙、山凹和一些缓坡山地，以石砌梯，填土建园；也有的利用竣险石隙，砌筑石座，运填客土，以蓄名丛；还有的利用天然石缝寄植茶树。这种盆栽式茶园的基础建设十分漫长，非一朝一夕之功，由唐宋至今，历千余年之久，是数百代武夷山茶农辛勤劳作的结果。20世纪50年代以后，武夷山茶事复兴，绝大部分茶园都是垦复栽植。

◎ 水金龟。（郑友裕 摄）

Golden Water Turtle. (Photo by Zheng Youyu)

◎ 铁罗汉。（郑友裕 摄）

Iron Arhat. (Photo by Zheng Youyu)

Mount Wuyi is known as "the kingdom of tea varieties". Tea people of all times devoted themselves to exploring and breeding a variety of famous teas from natural wild tea seeds. From the Song Dynasty to the Ming Dynasty, and then to the peak period of Wuyi Rock Tea in the late Qing Dynasty, Mount Wuyi gave birth to "four famous teas"—Tieluohan (Iron Arhat, Song Dynasty), Baijiguan (White Cockscomb, Ming Dynasty), Dahongpao (Big Red Robe, Mid-Qing Dynasty) and Shuijingui (Golden Water Turtle, the early years of Republic of China). There are also Bantianyao, Buzhichun, Jinsuoshi (Gold Key), Bairuixiang, Baimudan (White Peony), Shuixian (Narcissus), Rougui (Cinnamon) and other precious species.

The unique potted tea plantations (plantations) in Mount Wuyi are also different from those of other tea areas. Since most of the tea growing area here has a complicated terrain, the mountainous tea fields are built in valleys, deep pits, rock crevices, coves and some gentle slopes, using stones to build walls and filling them with soil to form gardens. Also, some utilize stone gaps and piles to build stone bases, then fill them with gravel and earth to cultivate the famous tea. Others use natural stone crevices to plant tea trees. The construction of the potted tea plantation infrastructure took a long time. It's been going on for more than 1,000 years since the Tang and Song dynasties and is the result of the hard work of many generations of tea farmers in Mount Wuyi. After the 1950s, Mount Wuyi underwent a tea renaissance, and many under-utilized tea plantations were reclaimed and cultivated.

◎ 武夷山盆栽式茶园。（郑友裕 摄）
The potted tea plantation in Mount Wuyi. (Photo by Zheng Youyu)

◎ 采摘。（郑友裕 摄）
Picking tea leaves. (Photo by Zheng Youyu)

武夷岩茶的传统制作技艺

　　武夷岩茶传统手工制作技艺历史悠久，手艺精湛，有"武夷焙法，实甲天下"之美誉。其工序之繁复，技艺之高超，劳动强度之大，费时之长，制约因素之多，令人叹为观止。茶界泰斗陈椽曾概括性地评价说："武夷岩茶的创制技术独一无二，为全世界最先进的技术，无与伦比，值得中国劳动人民雄视世界。"2006年，武夷岩茶（大红袍）制作技艺被列入第一批《国家级非物质文化遗产代表性项目名录》（传统技艺类）。

　　武夷岩茶（大红袍）传统制作技艺流程包括：采摘→萎凋【晒青→晾青（复式萎凋即二晒二晾）】→做青【摇青与做手（反复多次）】→炒青→揉捻（双炒双揉）→初焙（即毛火，俗称"走水焙）→扬簸→晾索（摊放）→拣剔→复焙（足火）→团包→补火→毛茶→装箱。

　　这过程看似可以用工整的文字罗列，但其中奥秘，全部在于匠人的手与心之间。好的制茶师傅，对于茶青的品种、所在山场、生长过程中经历的天气变化等了然于心，在制茶的过程中给予有针对性的调整与弥补，这种独一无二的经验，才是武夷岩茶的珍贵所在。

　　每年的4月下旬到5月中旬是武夷山的制茶季。如果你愿意，不妨于此间多抽一些日子来体验一下茶季的"茶修之旅"：从与人、与茶、与土地的连接，到跟随茶树叶子的节奏，沿着武夷岩茶制作技艺的脉络，亲手参与每一个工序。当你静下心来，就能够深入其中，"触摸"到茶，从青叶到杯中香茗，体会一种人茶合一的境界。也许茶修后，你会决定回家之后好好喝茶。

◎ 日光萎凋。（郑友裕 摄）
Sun withering. (Photo by Zheng Youyu)

◎ 做青。（宋春 摄）
Tossing the tea leaves. (Photo by Song Chun)

Traditional Producing Techniques of Wuyi Rock Tea

Using exquisite craftsmanship, traditional handmade techniques of Wuyi Rock Tea have a long history and enjoy the reputation of "the best tea baking method in the world". The complexity of the process and refining factors, the superb skills, the labor intensity, the time-consuming nature, are all breathtaking. Chen Chuan, a leading figure in the tea industry, has generally commented that, "Wuyi Rock Tea creation technology is unique. It is the world's most advanced and unparalleled technology." In 2006, Wuyi Rock Tea (Dahongpao) producing techniques were listed as one of the representative items of the national intangible cultural heritage (traditional handicraft techniques).

Wuyi Rock Tea (Dahongpao) traditional producing techniques involve: picking→withering [sun wilting→tea leaves airing (double withering)]→laying leaves including setting and tossing [stirring and lapping by hand (repeatedly)]→stirring fixation→rolling (double stirring and rolling)→roasting (i.e. first firing, commonly known as "moisture removal")→winnowing→drying in the air (to form natural twist tightness)→de-stemming→re-roasting (full fire)→sub-packaging→complement of firing→primary tea→packaging.

On the surface this process can be described in neat words, but the secret lies in the hands and skills of the craftsmen. A good tea maker knows the variety of fresh leaves, the mountain fields where they are from, and the changes of weather experienced during their growth. He will make key adjustments and compensations during the process of tea making (much like a good wine maker). Such unique craftsmanship is the charming distinction of Wuyi Rock Tea.

The tea making season in Mount Wuyi is from late April to mid-May every year. If you like, take some days to experience the journey of "tea cultivation" during the tea season: from the connection with people, tea and land to the rhythm of the tea leaves, you can personally participate in each process. If you calm your mind down, you may go deeper into it and "feel" the tea, from green leaves to the tea in the cup, and experience a kind of unity between tea, man and nature. Maybe after this experience, you will know how to enjoy the tea better when you get home.

◎ 炒青。（郑友裕 摄）

Stirring the tea leaves. (Photo by Zheng Youyu)

◎ 手工揉捻。（郑友裕 摄）

Rolling the tea leaves by hand. (Photo by Zheng Youyu)

◎ 镌刻着《茶说》的石碑。（宋春 摄）

The stone tablet engraved with *Tea Talk*. (Photo by Song Chun)

被誉为"乌龙茶问世记证人"的清代布衣文士王草堂在《茶说》中详细记述了武夷岩茶的采摘与制作过程：

"武夷茶自谷雨采至立夏，谓之头春；约隔二旬复采，谓之二春；又隔又采，谓之三春。头春叶粗味浓，二春三春叶渐细，味渐薄，且带苦矣。夏末秋初又采一次，名为秋露，香更浓，味亦佳，但为来年计，惜之，不能多采耳。茶采后以竹筐匀铺，架于风日中，名曰晒青。俟其色青渐收，然后再加炒焙。阳羡岕片只蒸不炒，火焙以成。松萝、龙井皆炒而不焙，故其色纯。独武夷炒焙兼施，烹出之时半青半红，青者乃炒色，红者乃焙色也。茶采而摊，摊而摝，香气发越即炒，经时、不及皆不可。既炒既焙，复拣去其中老叶枝蒂，使之一色。释超全诗云：'如梅斯馥兰斯馨，心闲手敏工夫细。'形容殆尽矣。"

"心闲手敏工夫细"，武夷岩茶制作过程中，最迷人的莫过于这种人与茶的"亲密接触"。各种发生于茶叶上的细微变化，需要你以从容的心态默默关注，并与之适时互动。拿传统炭焙工艺的工序来说，师傅们每半小时就要翻拌一次，闻香，察色。时间久了，人与茶之间，会产生一种宛若情人的连接，就连那些器具，看起来都有一种温润之感。

传统制作技艺中使用的工具多取自天然。再拿传统炭焙工艺来说，焙窟为土、石搭建，焙铲、焙刀、炭勺为铁制品，焙笼、焙筛、拖枋为竹篾制品，披灰刀为木制品，热能也取自天然炭薪。

佳茗自然天成，正是："天有时，地有气，材有美，工有巧，合此四者，然后可以为良。"

◎ 传统炭焙。（宋春 摄）

Traditional charcoal baking. (Photo by Song Chun)

◎ 炭焙工具。（宋春 摄）

Tools for charcoal baking. (Photo by Song Chun)

Qing Dynasty scribe Wang Caotang, "witness of the emergence of oolong tea", described in detail the process of picking and making Wuyi Rock Tea in his book *Tea Talk*:

"The picking time of Wuyi tea is from the Grain Rain (6th solar term) to the Beginning of Summer (7th solar term)—that is the first spring; about twenty days later tea farmers pick again—the second spring; another twenty days, pick again—the third spring. The tea leaves in the first spring are thick and have strong flavor; the leaves are gradually thinner, and the taste is bitterer in the second and third spring pickings. In the late summer and early autumn, they pick again, called autumn dew. This time the fragrance is thicker, and the flavor is good, but to protect the tea trees for the next year, they can't pick too much. After picking, they spread the tea leaves evenly on a large flat bamboo basket, prop it up in the wind and sun—this is called sun withering. When the green color has faded, then roast. Yangxian Jie Tea is only steamed without stir-frying and baked on the fire. Songluo, Longjing are fried and not baked, so they have pure color. Only Wuyi Rock Tea is fried and roasted to present half green and half red. Green is the frying color; red is the roasted color. Pick, spread, roll and fry when the aroma gives out. Don't be too early or too late. After frying and roasting, remove the old leaves and twigs, and make them one color. Shi Chaoquan has a poem to describe the process, 'Such is the fragrance of plum and orchid—it needs a quiet heart, quick hands and care. That's a good description.'"

In the process of making Wuyi Rock Tea, the most charming thing is the close contact between man and tea and nature. All kinds of subtle changes occur during the processing of the tea, so you need to keep calm, pay attention and interact timely—like an artisan. Take the process of traditional charcoal baking for example. The masters turn and mix tea leaves every half hour to smell the aroma and observe the color. Over a long period of time, this interaction between craftsperson and tea produces a special connection, a connected feeling even with the equipment.

In traditional manufacturing techniques, tools are often taken from nature. In the traditional charcoal baking process, the broiling caves are built of soil and stones, the broiling shovels, knives and charcoal spoons are made of iron; the cages, broiling sieves and utensils are made of bamboo sticks; the ash knives are made of wood; and finally the heat is also derived from natural charcoal.

The best tea is made by nature, which means: "Heaven picks the right time, the earth provides the energy, the material has its own beauty, and the craftsman is highly skilled—combine these four, and then it may become a work of the gods."

◎ 春茶丰收。（郑友裕 摄）
The spring tea harvest. (Photo by Zheng Youyu)

作为自然与技艺天人合一的产物，武夷岩茶与众不同的制作工艺无疑会反映在茶叶的品质上。"绿叶红镶边（三红七绿），七泡有余香（经久耐泡），汤色橙黄（呈琥珀色），清澈艳丽，叶底明亮，香气馥郁，滋味醇厚鲜爽，回甘韵显，润滑爽口"是对武夷岩茶品质的教科书式定义。

著名的茶叶专家廖存仁在《武夷岩茶》一书中则写道："（武夷岩茶）品具岩骨花香之胜，制法介乎红茶、绿茶之间，必求所谓'绿叶红镶边'者，方称上乘，性和不寒，久藏不坏，香久益清，味久益醇，味甘泽，而气馥郁，无绿茶之苦涩，有红茶之浓艳。"

岩骨花香，为武夷茶之岩韵真味。

As a product of the integration of nature and man, Wuyi Rock Tea's distinctive producing techniques will be reflected in the quality of tea. "Green leaves with red edge (30% red and 70% green), after brewing even for seven times it still retains a fine lingering fragrance (a lasting taste). The color of the tea is orange and yellow (amber), clear and gorgeous; the leaves at the bottom are bright; the aroma is fragrant; the taste is mellow and fresh; the flavor is sweet, clear, and refreshing"—this is the textbook definition of the quality of Wuyi Rock Tea.

Liao Cunren, a famous tea expert, wrote in the book *Wuyi Rock Tea*, "(Wuyi Rock Tea) wins with rock bone and flower fragrance. The techniques are between those of making black tea and green tea, with the so-called 'green leaves with red edge' being the best. It is mild and doesn't contain 'cold' energy; it can keep for a long time and doesn't spoil; the aroma is fresh and lasting; the taste is mellow and lingers long; the flavor is sweet and fragrant with the intensity of black tea, but not the bitterness of green tea."

Rock bone and flower fragrance—the special unique flavor of Wuyi Rock Tea.

◎ 绿叶红镶边。（宋春 摄）
Green leaves with red edge. (Photo by Song Chun)

◎ 茶园晨光。（宋春 摄）
Early morning sunshine in the tea plantation. (Photo by Song Chun)

武夷岩茶精湛的传统制作技艺是历代劳动人民的智慧结晶。种茶、制茶与武夷山人的生活息息相关，千年的传承催生了一些与茶相关的民间仪式和艺术创作。

据史料记载，唐代已开始栽制茶叶的武夷山民间，每年春茶开采前都要举行"开山"等祭拜仪式，祈求茶事顺遂、增产丰收。

采摘开始之日，俗称为"开山"，一般定于立夏前二三日。正式开山采摘之日，按武夷山习俗，茶厂工人黎明起床，不得言语，漱洗完毕，由茶厂的工头开始，依次在厂中供奉的武夷山制茶祖师杨太白的神位前焚香行礼，然后进山，分散采茶。待到太阳升起、露水初收之时，工头示意之后，大家才可以自由说话。

现在仍有一些茶厂举行开山仪式，只是开山采茶的日期已提前至4月中旬左右，远早于立夏。

The unique traditional production techniques of Wuyi Rock Tea are largely due to the cumulative wisdom of generations of working people. Tea planting and tea making are closely related to the life of Mount Wuyi people, and thousands of years of heritage has given birth to many tea-related folk rituals and artistic creations.

According to historical records, people in Mount Wuyi began to plant and produce tea during the Tang Dynasty. Every year, before the spring tea was picked, they would hold worship ceremonies such as "Kaishan (Opening the mountains)" to pray for a smooth tea harvest and plentiful production.

The day when the picking begins is commonly known as "Kaishan", which is usually set at two or three days before the Beginning of Summer (7th solar term). On the day of the official opening of the mountains for picking, according to the custom of Mount Wuyi, the tea factory workers get up at dawn but cannot speak. After they wash their faces and rinse their mouths, starting with the foreman, everyone burns incense and bows in front of the sacred position of Yang Taibai (the ancestor of tea making) enshrined in the factory, and then they enter the mountain and spread out to pick tea. When the sun rises and the dew begins to evaporate, the foreman signals, and only then is everyone free to speak.

Today, some tea factories still hold such traditional ceremonies to open the mountain, but the date has been brought forward to around mid-April, much earlier than the Beginning of Summer.

◎ 祭茶祈福仪式。（郑友裕 摄）
The worship ceremony for a tea harvest. (Photo by Zheng Youyu)

采茶歌是由采茶工们在劳作与休息时即兴吟唱而成，有的经文人润色，在乡间广泛传唱。一些上了年纪的老茶工，现在劳作时依然喜欢哼唱那些古老的茶歌。

被称为"植物猎人""茶盗"的英国植物学家罗伯特·福琼在《两访中国茶乡》中写道："当我们在山里钻来钻去的时候，我们看到采茶的人们正在山坡上的茶园里忙着采茶，他们似乎正在进行一场快乐而又心满意足的比赛，互相开着玩笑，到处充满快乐的笑声，还有一些人在唱歌，就像庙里那些古树上的鸟儿一样高兴。"

与之形成对比的是，明代吴栻的诗里却这样写道："茶歌音最凄婉，每一声从云际飘来，令人潜然堕泪，吴歌未必能动人如此也。"

同样的场景，同样的茶人，为什么不同旁观者的感受如此大相径庭呢？或许，在武夷山这样的丹山碧水之间劳作，从视觉上，的确是一幅诗意的田园画，然而，这画中之人，又何尝没有自己的酸甜苦辣？有一首茶歌这样唱道："武夷山上茶厂多，哪个茶工不唱歌。包头说我好快活，眼睛爱睏无奈何。"这首茶歌真实反映了制茶季的辛苦，茶工几乎天天熬夜。所以武夷山的女制茶师非常少也是有原因的。武夷山人常打趣说，要想瘦啊，去做茶。

每一片茶叶都来之不易，且喝且珍惜。

Tea-picking songs are impromptu songs sung by tea-picking workers during their work and rest. Some of the songs have been embellished by literati and widely sung in the countryside. Some old tea workers still like to sing the old tea songs when they are working.

Referred to as the "plant hunter" and "tea thief", English botanist Robert Fortune wrote in *Two Visits to the Tea Countries of China*, "When we were walking in the mountains, we saw the tea picking people busy picking tea on the hillside. They seemed to be in a happy and contented mood, joking with each other, full of happy laughter. Some were singing like the happy birds on the ancient trees."

By contrast, Wu Shi in the Ming Dynasty wrote a poem, "Tea songs are the most sympathetic; each sound from the clouds moves people to tears …"

The same scene, the same tea workers, why do different onlookers feel so different? Perhaps, from the visual point of view, it is indeed a poetic pastoral painting to have men and women work and sing between mountains and waters like Mount Wuyi. However, the people in this painting have their own sweet and bitter life. There is a tea song that goes like this, "There are many tea factories in Mount Wuyi; every tea worker sings a tea song. The foreman said we were happy, but I sing simply because I felt drowsy in my eyes (tired)." This tea song really sings about the painstaking work during the tea making season. Tea workers stay up almost every day. This is the reason why there are so few female tea masters. People in Mount Wuyi often joke that if you want to be thin, just go make tea.

Every piece of tea is not easy to make—so cherish it when you drink the tea.

© 岩下采茶。（郑友裕 摄）
Picking tea leaves by a cliff. (Photo by Zheng Youyu)

◎ 武夷岩茶茶干。（宋春 摄）
Dry Wuyi Rock Tea. (Photo by Song Chun)

带人到无上妙境里

武夷岩茶是乌龙茶中的珍品，以讲究内质为特色。品尝武夷岩茶是一件极富诗意的雅事，自古以来，文人学士都非常崇尚这种口腹与精神的双重享受。品尝武夷岩茶讲究环境、心境、茶具、水质、冲泡技巧和品饮艺术。

清代文学家、美食家袁枚在《随园食单·茶酒单》中，对品饮武夷岩茶有一段生动的描写：

"余向不喜武夷茶，嫌其浓苦如饮药。然丙午秋，余游武夷，到幔亭峰、天游寺诸处，僧道争以茶献。杯小如胡桃，壶小如香橼，每斟无一两。上口不忍遽咽，先嗅其香，再试其味，徐徐咀嚼而体贴之，果然清芬扑鼻，舌有余甘。一杯之后，再试一二杯，令人释躁平矜，怡情悦性。始觉龙井虽清而味薄矣，阳羡虽佳而韵逊矣，颇有玉与水晶，品格不同之故。故武夷享天下盛名，真乃不忝。"

小杯、小壶，先嗅香，再试味，慢慢品味感受清香回甘，正是地道的武夷岩茶品饮方法。而"释躁平矜，怡情悦性"则把品饮武夷岩茶提升到了艺术层面，视其为一种精神享受和修身养性之法。身处武夷，可享山水之乐，品武夷岩茶，可至无上妙境，难怪武夷山会成为儒、释、道三教的圣地以及奇人、雅士、归隐官员聚集的地方。如果真的可以穿越到古代，你在武夷山随便走一走，碰上某位僧道、樵夫、茶农，可都不要小觑，保不准他就是今天历史书上的大名人呢。

◎ 武夷岩茶的琥珀汤色。（宋春　摄）
The amber soup of Wuyi Rock Tea. (Photo by Song Chun)

◎ 武夷岩茶的蛙皮状叶底。（宋春　摄）
The sopped tea leaves like frog skin. (Photo by Song Chun)

Bringing Man to a Wonderful Place

Wuyi Rock Tea is the high point of oolong tea, which is characterized by its inner quality. Tasting Wuyi Rock Tea can be a poetic and elegant experience. Since ancient times, scholars have been advocating this kind of double enjoyment of taste and spirit. The environment, the mood, the tea set, the water quality, the brewing skills and the art of tasting tea are all integral parts for enjoying Wuyi Rock Tea.

Yuan Mei, a writer and gourmet in the Qing Dynasty, gave a vivid description of drinking Wuyi Rock Tea:

"I didn't like Wuyi Tea; however, in the autumn of 1786, I went to visit the Manting Peak, Tianyou Temple and some other places in Mount Wuyi, and the monks and priests all wanted me to drink the tea. The cup is as small as a walnut; the pot is small and fragrant like oak; in each cup there is less than 50ml, and I held off swallowing when it was in my mouth in order to savor the taste. Smell its fragrance first, taste a little bit, slowly move it around in your mouth and sense it, and behold, sure enough, the palate is sweet and pleasant. After one cup, try one or two cups more, and it will release the mania and bring unique pleasure. Then I start to think about the Longjing Tea which is clear, but the taste is thin; the Yangxian Tea which is good but the rhythm is poor—quite like the character difference between the jade and crystal. Therefore, Wuyi enjoys a good reputation for its tea in the world; that's true."

Small cups, small pots, first smelling fragrance, then tasting, slowly savoring the fragrance all the way through to the pleasant aftertaste—this is the authentic Wuyi Rock Tea tasting ceremony. "Release the mania and bring unique pleasure" elevates drinking Wuyi Rock Tea to an artistic level, regarding it as an experience of spiritual enjoyment and self-cultivation. It is no wonder that Mount Wuyi has become the holy land of Confucianism, Buddhism and Taoism as well as the gathering place of special people, scholars and reclusive officials. If you can travel back through the time tunnel and take a walk in the ancient Mount Wuyi, maybe you will meet a monk, a woodcutter, or an old tea farmer. Be alert! He may be one of the historical figures from the history books.

◎ 武夷岩茶茶席。（郑友裕 摄）
The placement of Wuyi Rock Tea. (Photo by Zheng Youyu)

◎ 外国游客品饮武夷岩茶。（郑友裕 摄）
Foreign tourists enjoying Wuyi Rock Tea. (Photo by Zheng Youyu)

◎《印象大红袍》演出。（郑友裕 摄）
The performance of *Impression Dahongpao*. (Photo by Zheng Youyu)

　　如今到武夷山的旅行者，不可错过的体验除了喝岩茶、品岩韵之外，还有一场高水准的艺术盛宴——《印象大红袍》。它是由2008年北京奥运会开幕式总导演张艺谋和核心创意小组成员王潮歌、樊跃倾力打造的"印象系列"作品之一，是以世界文化与自然双重遗产胜地武夷山为舞台背景、以武夷茶文化为表现主题的大型山水实景演出。演出巧妙地把自然景观、茶文化及民俗文化融为一体，观众置身于山水实景间，坐在世界上视觉总长度第一、5分钟即可完成一次360度平稳旋转的舞台上欣赏如梦似幻的艺术表演，不得不说是一次奇妙的体验。出人意料的是，参与这华美演出的接近300个演员并不都是专业演员出身，他们当中90%是武夷山当地人，有人是土生土长的农民，有人是九曲溪上筏工的女儿，有人是会说几句英语的导游。如今，他们用另外一种方式来展示家乡之美，起初这可能只是一份工作，演着演着，不经意之间，他们就把自己对生活的理解，对家人的爱，对这一方山水的感恩与眷恋，都融入其中了。

In addition to drinking Wuyi Rock Tea and appreciating the tea culture, there is also a high-quality visual performance for you to enjoy, *Impression Dahongpao*. It is one of the "impression series" works created by Zhang Yimou, chief director of the opening ceremony of the 2008 Beijing Olympic Games, and also Wang Chaoge and Fan Yue, members of the core creative team. It is a large-scale stage performance with Mount Wuyi as the stage background and Wuyi tea culture as the theme. The performance skillfully integrates the natural landscape, tea culture and folk culture. The audience can enjoy the dreamlike artistic performance by sitting on a moving platform with a steady rotation of 360 degrees every 5 minutes. It is really a wonderful experience. Surprisingly, most of the nearly 300 actors who take part in the extravaganza, 90 percent anyway, are natives of Mount Wuyi, some are native farmers, some are the daughters of rafts men on Nine-Bend Stream, and some are tour guides who speak a few words of English. Now, they use another platform to showcase the beauty of their hometown. It may have been just a job in the beginning, but after they started acting, inadvertently, they put their own understanding of life, love for their family, gratitude and attachment to the landscape, all into it.

◎ 《印象大红袍》演出。（苏永青 摄）
The performance of *Impression Dahongpao*. (Photo by Su Yongqing)

茶日子 日日是好日

■ 大茶壶

中国的茶，在"琴棋书画诗酒茶"里是风雅，而在"柴米油盐酱醋茶"的平常日子里亦不可缺少。

在武夷山，早年还能在寻常百姓家见到大茶壶冲泡的粗片茶，是平日里用来解渴之物。喝粗片茶，用一种纯朴的接受的态度细细体会它纯正的滋味，能帮助你从茶树叶子的本质上去认知茶。

如今用大茶壶泡茶已不多见，倒是在一些茶会所还能看见大茶壶的身影，已成一种摆设。在武夷山当地，还有一位姓卓的老师傅在做这样的大茶壶，因为做得多、做得久了，整个制作过程，流淌着一种真实自在之美。

卓师傅年少时，身为家中长子，要担起养家糊口的责任，故而从父亲那里承接了这门手艺。这一做，就是一辈子。

而今，这手艺褪去了生计的成分，却变成生命里不可缺少的养心良方。匠人，透过手艺，用一生实践着"以手代心"的生活哲学，未尝不是一种禅的意境。

透过器物，看见此种禅意，恰是体会器物之美之时。

◎ 大茶壶。（宋春 摄）
The big teapot. (Photo by Song Chun)

Every Day Is a Good Day When Accompanied by Tea

The Big Teapot

For Chinese, tea is an integral part of the "zither, chess, calligraphy, painting, poetry, wine and tea" (an ancient expression of a refined life), but in the ordinary day of "firewood, rice, oil, salt, sauce, vinegar and tea", tea is also part of the daily ritual of Chinese life.

In the early years, coarse tea brewed by big teapots could be seen in ordinary people's homes in Mount Wuyi, which was used to quench their daily thirst. Drinking coarse tea, with a simple acceptance of its pure taste can help you to understand the essence of tea leaves.

Nowadays, making coarse tea this way with a big teapot is not often seen. However, the figure of a big teapot has become a common decoration in some tea chambers. In Mount Wuyi, there is an old master surnamed Zhuo, who is still making such big teapots. Because he has made so many and made them for so long, his whole shop is full of a genuine beauty.

When master Zhuo was young, he was the eldest son of the family, and he was responsible for supporting the family. So he took over the craft from his father. It has been his lifetime work.

Although this skill has lost its critical aspect as a livelihood, it is still an indispensable ingredient of his life. The craftsmen, through their craft, practice the life philosophy of "substituting the heart with the hand" during their whole life—this is another Zen-tea realm.

When you see the "Tao" in the condiments, you know where beauty lies.

◎ 烧制民间器具的柴窑。（宋春 摄）
The wood kiln for firing folk wares. (Photo by Song Chun)

■ 木印糕子

一个地方的本土风物，会有一种向下扎根的力量，使人得以与这片山水愈发紧密联结起来。在武夷山，能让你体会到这种感觉的，除了大茶壶这样的茶器，还有传统木印糕子这样的吃食。木印糕子，是把米、花生等原料炒好磨碎，拌入白糖、芝麻，放入形状、花纹各异的模子里，手工填满，敲打结实，再倒扣出来，用木炭烤干而成。"炒粉调糖扑鼻香，年年岁末印糕忙。小儿最算他无赖，未待烘干入口尝。"说的就是武夷山的木印糕子。

早年间的糕子，是过年时才有的好东西，小口咬下去，在嘴里慢慢嚼，能品到纯粹的米香。如今，日日是好日，很少有什么东西是要等到过年才吃得到的。木印糕子用来做茶点倒是很好，不会夺茶味。细嚼慢咽，和着茶的幽远韵味，不急不缓，有一种好玩的节奏在其间。

茶、器、糕等等这些风物，仿佛在说：造物要人沉静自爱。

■ Wooden-Mold Cake

The native features of a place create a downward rooting force, making people more closely connected with this land. In Mount Wuyi, in addition to vessels such as big teapots, there are also local foods that make you sense this feeling, such as the traditional Wooden-Mold Cake, which is made of fried and ground rice, peanuts, sugar, sesame seeds and other raw materials. The villagers put the mixture into molds with different shapes and patterns, fill them up manually, hammer them firmly, invert the cakes and roast them to dry over charcoal. There is a poem about the Wooden-Mold Cake: "Stir-fried flour mixed with sugar has tangy scent; adults are busy making cakes at the end of the year. The children are naughty; they go taste the cakes when they have not yet dried."

In the early years, the Wooden-Mold Cake was a favorite food during the Spring Festival; take a small bite, slowly chew in the mouth, and taste its pure rice flavor. Nowadays, every day is a good day. There are very few things you can't eat until Chinese New Year. The Wooden-Mold Cake becomes a good refreshment when you drink tea, because it never steals the flavor of tea. Chew slowly and swallow it, with the lingering charm of tea; there is an interesting rhythm, not urgent and not slow.

Tea, utensils, cakes, and so on, seem to say, "Hand-making brings calmness and contentment."

◎ 木印糕子模具。（宋春 摄）

The wooden molds for making cakes. (Photo by Song Chun)

◎ 木印糕子。（宋春 摄）

Cakes made with wooden molds. (Photo by Song Chun)

■ 茶百戏

茶百戏又称分茶、水丹青，风行于两宋时期，是古代点茶、斗茶文化的重要技艺。

北宋陶谷在《荈茗录》中对茶百戏这种民间游艺有过记载："茶至唐始盛，近世有下汤运匕，别施妙诀，使汤纹水脉成物象者。禽兽虫鱼花草之属，纤巧如画，但须臾即就散灭。此茶之变也，时人谓茶百戏。""下汤运匕"即汤瓶注汤和茶勺搅动，看似简单的两个动作，经过技艺高超的师傅细腻拿捏，汤纹水脉即可幻变出各种图案，茶中有画，画中有诗。

有些游客觉得茶百戏和咖啡拉花异曲同工，其实二者在历史背景、显像原理、图案持久度等等方面都有本质上的不同。茶百戏是借助茶汤泡沫，用清水幻变图案，光是碾茶一个步骤，就需要许多技巧，在茶汤上作画也体现着个人的技艺和感悟。茶百戏呈现出来的是一种朦胧之美，非常适合展示中国水墨画风格的山水佳人、花鸟虫鱼、重峦叠嶂、炊烟袅袅。

茶百戏已被列为福建省非物质文化遗产项目。

◎ 茶筅击拂。（郑友裕 摄）

Stirring the tea soup with a bamboo whisk. (Photo by Zheng Youyu)

◎ 茶百戏传承人章志峰，经过二十多年的研究和实践使已经失传的茶百戏技艺得到抢救性恢复。
（郑友裕 摄）
Zhang Zhifeng, inheritor of tea acrobatics, who regained the techniques after more than twenty years' research and practice. (Photo by Zheng Youyu)

■ Chabaixi (Tea Acrobatics)

Tea acrobatics, also known as tea pouring painting, became popular in the Song Dynasty. It was a refined skill in the ancient tea competition culture.

In the Northern Song Dynasty Tao Gu recorded this folk tea practice, "Tea began to flourish in the Tang Dynasty. Recently someone can pour the tea soup in a bowl and stir with a spoon to make the ripples of tea soup and water form paintings on the surface. Animals, insects, fish, flowers and plants are all delicate and picturesque, but disperse quickly. People call the images and changes on the surface of tea 'tea acrobatics'." Pouring out the tea soup , then stirring with a spoon—with two seemingly simple movements, the ripples of the tea and water can be conjured into various images by a skilled master, like poetry in a painting.

Some visitors feel that tea acrobatics and coffee latte art have the same style. In fact, they are fundamentally different in historical background, display principle, pattern persistence and so on. To create patterns with water and bubbles of the tea liquid, tea acrobatics requires a host of skills starting from the very beginning—grinding the tea. Painting on the tea liquid also displays a unique technique, which relies on one's own skills and feelings. Tea acrobatics show a hazy beauty, which is suitable for displaying landscapes, flowers, birds, insects, fish, mountains and smoke curling up from kitchen chimneys—like the style of Chinese ink paintings.

Tea acrobatics has been listed as an intangible cultural heritage of Fujian Province.

◎ 茶百戏作品——人物。（章志峰 供图）
Tea acrobatics—the figure of a beautiful woman. (Courtesy of Zhang Zhifeng)

◎ 茶百戏作品——风景和动物。（章志峰 供图）
Tea acrobatics—the scenery and animals. (Courtesy of Zhang Zhifeng)

■ 麻糍粿

"幔亭招宴"的传说不仅衍生出武夷山各大酒店最具传奇色彩的特色神仙宴——幔亭宴，还使一道来自乡野百姓家的传统美食流传下来，那就是胡麻饭。在不少武夷山的神话传说中，神仙都用胡麻饭招待乡人，故而被称为"神仙饭"，民间也称其为麻糍粿。麻糍粿入口爽滑细腻，嚼劲十足，如今是乡村宴席中简单古朴的美味。

将糯米用水浸泡一夜之后，捞起来放入饭甑里蒸熟，倒入石臼中，用木杵捶打，使米粒完全融合，变成柔软棉絮状，搓成一小团一小团的，放到炒熟碾碎和加了糖的芝麻里滚，糯、甜、香、滑的麻糍粿就做成了。

◎ 外国游客品尝麻糍粿。（郑友裕 摄）
Foreign visitors tasting Maci Cake. (Photo by Zheng Youyu)

◎ 打麻糍粿。（郑友裕 摄）

Beating the glutinous rice to make Maci Cake. (Photo by Zheng Youyu)

Maci Cake

The legend of "Manting banquet" not only enlightens the hotels in Wuyishan to cook the legendary immortal banquet—Manting banquet, but also makes a traditional local delicacy made with glutinous rice, Maci Cake, popular. In many myths and legends of Mount Wuyi, immortals entertain villagers with the food, so it is called "immortals' rice", also known as Maci Cake. Smooth and chewy, the glutinous dish is a simple, rustic delicacy at local banquets.

This is how it is made: soak the glutinous rice overnight, scoop it out and steam it, pour it into a stone mortar, and beat with a wooden pestle. When the rice grains are completely fused and become soft and cotton-like, make small balls and roll them in crushed sesame seeds mixed with sugar—the glutinous, sweet, fragrant and smooth Maci Cake is ready.

◎ 光饼制作。（郑友裕 摄）
Making Guang Cake. (Photo by Zheng Youyu)

■ 光饼

　　戚继光在武夷山不仅写下了直抒胸臆的诗句，还在民间留下了一样日常小吃，那就是光饼。相传戚继光当年带兵围剿倭寇时发明此饼，后人谓之"光饼"。这道小吃在武夷山传承了400多年，连很多外国游客都特地寻访品尝。光饼是用面粉制成面团，取适量大小裹上肉馅，放进烤炉内烘烤。烤熟后的面饼焦香、酥脆、美味，是闽北人日常爱吃的零食之一。

　　武夷山市区有一位老孙师傅做光饼30多年了，他的光饼就叫"俺老孙光饼"，口味尤其地道。除了本地熟客来买，还经常有慕名而来的游客专程来找。光饼新鲜出炉时，热热乎乎最是好吃，在炉子边等着的时候，一边看孙师傅干活，一边和他聊天，也是件乐事。

　　孙师傅说他的光饼没啥秘诀，只遵循一个原则：做人诚信，舍得材料，从面粉到肉馅，甚至烤制的炭，都要用好料就是了。看孙师傅做光饼是种享受，每一个步骤都干净利落，却气韵流动，整个人洋溢着一种踏实和满足的感觉。以艺藏道，说的或许就是这种老百姓的日子了，恰如法国艺术家杜尚所言："我最好的作品，是我的生活。"

◎ 俺老孙光饼。（郑友裕 摄）

Cakes made by Master Sun. (Photo by Zheng Youyu)

Guang Cake

In Mount Wuyi, Qi Jiguang not only wrote poetry that expressed his feelings directly, but also left a daily snack with the folk villagers, the Guang Cake. Legend has it that Qi Jiguang invented this cake when he led troops to suppress Japanese pirates. This snack has been passed down in Wuyi area for more than 400 years, and even many foreign tourists have made special trips just to taste it. The Guang Cake is made of flour dough—take an appropriate size, fill it with meat stuffing, and then put it into the oven to bake. The baked cake is charred, crispy and delicious, which is one of the favorite snacks in northern Fujian.

In the urban area of Wuyishan City there is an old Master Sun, who has made these cakes for more than 30 years. The taste is especially authentic. In addition to the local regular customers, he also attracts many tourists to buy his cakes. When the cake is freshly baked, it is hot and delicious. While waiting by the stove, it's always a pleasure to watch Master Sun working and to chat with him.

Master Sun says there is no secret to his cakes, but only one principle: be honest and use only the best ingredients, from the flour to the meat and even the charcoal for baking. It is a joy to watch him make cakes. Every step is clean and neat, and a charm flows because his whole person is filled with a sense of sureness and satisfaction. There is "Tao" in a man's skills. This may be the life of ordinary people, as the French artist Duchamp said, "My best work is my life."

■ 文公菜

相传朱熹在治学之余颇好美食，常常自己动手制作。好友小酌，他制作的"什锦"获得交口称赞，很快便在乡村流传。因为朱熹谥号为"文公"，所以此菜后来又被称作"文公菜"。文公菜在武夷山民间代代相传，这里的学子大考前夕，家人必备此菜，祈愿考生才思敏捷，榜上有名。如今，文公菜已成为当地人宴请贵客的传统名菜，原料为猪精肉、精粉、鸡蛋、白扁豆，味道可口，营养丰富。

■ Wengong Dish

Legend has it that Zhu Xi often made his own food after studying. When friends came around for drinks, his "assorted dish" was praised and its fame soon spread through the countryside. It came to be known as Wengong Dish because of his posthumous title. Wengong Dish has been handed down from generation to generation in Mount Wuyi. It is a must-have dish for students there before they take an important exam, praying that their thinking is sharp and they get a good score. Nowadays, it has become a traditional dish for local people to entertain distinguished guests. The raw materials are lean pork, fine powder, eggs and white lentils, which are delicious and nutritious.

◎ 文公菜。（郑友裕 摄）
Wengong Dish. (Photo by Zheng Youyu)

◎ 岚谷熏鹅。（郑友裕 摄）

Langu Smoked Goose. (Photo by Zheng Youyu)

■ 武夷四宝

武夷山有四宝：东笋、西鱼、南茶、北米。

东笋产于武夷山市东路的上梅乡金竹村、首阳村一带，质嫩色白，清脆味甜，新鲜笋片拿来做汤，鲜美至极，笋干也颇受人们喜爱。

西鱼指的是出自武夷山市西路洋庄乡区域河流里的鲜鱼，只需以盐为作料，即可烹制出诱人美味，吃起来肉嫩味甜。

南茶即产于武夷山市南路武夷山景区范围的武夷岩茶。以武夷岩茶为配料制作的武夷茶宴心思巧妙，且有岩茶独特的清香与韵味，味清不腻，食之齿颊留香。

北米出自武夷山市北路的吴屯、岚谷两乡。这两地属于高山气候，因昼夜温差大，所产大米粒粒饱满，味道香醇。吴屯稻花鱼和岚谷熏鹅也是两道名气极大的武夷山美食。

◎ 笋王争霸赛上比孩童还高的东笋。（郑友裕 摄）
The king of East Bamboo Shoots even higher than kids. (Photo by Zheng Youyu)

◎ 武夷山北部的稻田。（郑友裕 摄）
The rice field in the northern Wuyishan City. (Photo by Zheng Youyu)

■ Wuyi Treasures

Mount Wuyi has four treasures: East Bamboo Shoots, West Fish, South Tea and North Rice.

East Bamboo Shoots are produced in Jinzhu and Shouyang villages of Shangmei Township in the eastern suburb of Wuyishan City. They are tender and white in color, crisp and sweet in taste. The fresh bamboo shoots can be used to make delicious soup, and dried bamboo shoots are also popular.

West Fish refers to fresh fish from the rivers in Yangzhuang Township in the western suburb of Wuyishan City. It only needs a little salt to cook, and the fish tastes sweet and tender.

South Tea is the Wuyi Rock Tea produced in Mount Wuyi Scenic Area in the southern suburb of Wuyishan City. The Wuyi tea banquet made with Wuyi Rock Tea as the ingredients is fantastic and has the unique fragrance and charm of rock tea. The taste is clear but not greasy, and the fragrance lingers in the mouth.

North Rice is from Wutun and Langu in the northern suburb of Wuyishan City. These two places enjoy a mountain climate, where the day and night temperature difference is large. So the rice grains are full, and the taste is mellow. Wutun Rice Field Fish and Langu Smoked Goose are also two famous Wuyi delicacies.

O3
旅行规划
Tours Recommended

◎ 烟雨天游峰。（郑友裕 摄）
Tianyou Peak in a misty rain. (Photo by Zheng Youyu.)

经典游一日线路

线路1：九曲溪竹筏漂流（沿途欣赏大藏峰、金鸡洞、笔架峰、鼓子峰、玉女峰、大王峰）→**宋街**（参观名人馆、三清殿、武夷宫）→**一曲止止庵**（观赏摩崖石刻）→**武夷精舍**→**云窝**→**茶洞**→**天游峰**（一览武夷山水，游隐屏峰、接笋峰、水月亭、晒布岩、天游阁、胡麻洞、中正公园等景点）

　　武夷山集山水之美于一身，有三十六峰、七十二洞、九十九岩，悠悠流淌的九曲碧水环绕其间，乘坐竹筏顺流而下，可观赏两岸山水与人文完美结合的画廊，山有气魄，水有大成，不仅"奇、秀、美、古"兼有，而且人文与自然达到和谐统一的绝妙境界。

　　一曲处下竹筏，可参观仿宋古街的自然博物馆，探索3,000多年前的船棺之谜。观赏武夷宫900多岁树龄的宋桂，而后漫步万春园，至一曲水光石、止止庵。水光石上有摩崖石刻共30余方，字体多样，情趣各异，内涵深广。

　　接下来乘车去天游景区，参访武夷精舍、云窝、茶洞，登顶天游峰远眺，山岳吞烟，河川静默，日月山河伴古今，尽显旷达之美。而天游峰胡麻洞处的30多方历代摩崖石刻，再次展示武夷山之人文光彩。

　　重拾用简单、自然的方式看世界的能力，在自然的祥和中凝神静气，天、地、人，和谐统一。

点评：

1. 这个行程凸显闲适旷达，在自然与人文中交错穿行，可尽情体会天、地、人之和谐。
2. 行程中包含九曲溪、天游峰等自然景观，是武夷山水的上乘之作。
3. 可看架壑船棺、武夷宫、止止庵以及众多摩崖石刻，饱览武夷山人文之美。

◎ 九曲泛舟。（郑友裕 摄）
Rafting on Nine-Bend Stream. (Photo by Zheng Youyu)

Classical Day-Trip Tours

Option 1: Nine-Bend Stream Rafting (Experience Dazang Peak, Jinji Cave, Bijia Peak, Guzi Peak, Jade Maiden Peak, and Great King Peak)→Song Dynasty Street (Visit the Hall of Fame, Sanqing Palace and Wuyi Academy)→Zhizhi Monastery at the first bend (View the inscriptions on the cliff wall)→Wuyi Academy→Cloud Nest→Tea Canyon→Tianyou Peak (An overview of the Wuyi mountains and rivers, enjoying Yinping Peak, Jiesun Peak, Shuiyue Pavilion, Shaibu Rock, Tianyou Pavilion, Huma Stream, Zhongzheng Park and more)

Mount Wuyi combines the beauty of mountains, flora, fauna and streams. It is said to have 36 peaks, 72 caves and 99 rocks. With the jade water of Nine-Bend Stream flowing slowly around them, you can enjoy the unique combination of nature and culture while rafting down the stream. The mountains have form, and the water has its own deeper significance (function). They are not only "beautiful and ancient", but they also achieve a perfect balance of harmony between man and nature.

After taking the bamboo raft down the stream, you can visit the Nature Museum in the Song Dynasty Historic Street and explore the mystery of the boat-shaped coffins (more than 3,000 years old). You can see an Osmanthus tree more than 900 years old from the Song Dynasty in Wuyi Palace, and then walk through Wanchun Garden to the Shuiguang Rock and Zhizhi Monastery at the first bend. There are more than 30 stone inscriptions on the cliff of Shuiguang Rock in a variety of styles, and with different meanings.

Then take a bus to the Tianyou Peak area, visit Wuyi Academy, Cloud Nest, Tea Canyon, and then climb to the top of Tianyou Peak to see as far as the eye can see—mountains swallowing mists, the silent streams, the sun and moon, all blending with each other from ancient times to now, all showing the beauty of a simple natural life. Here there are more than 30 cliff stone carvings from past dynasties along the Huma Stream at Tianyou Peak, which chronicle the cultural history of Mount Wuyi.

One can regain his ability to see the world in a simple and natural way—just focus on the tranquility of nature and enjoy the harmony between heaven, earth and man.

Comments:

1. This trip highlights leisure and mindfulness, just nature and man—relax and enjoy the harmony between heaven, earth … and yourself.

2. The trip includes Nine-Bend Stream, Tianyou Peak and other natural landscapes, which are among the best scenic spots of Mount Wuyi.

3. You can see the boat-shaped coffins, Wuyi Palace, Zhizhi Monastery and numerous cliff carvings, and enjoy the beauty and richness of the Mount Wuyi culture.

线路2： **岩骨花香慢游道**（大红袍母树→流香洞→慧苑寺→天车架）→**天心永乐禅寺→虎啸岩**（虎啸八景：白莲渡、集云关、坡仙带、普门兜、法雨悬河、语儿泉、不浪舟和宾曦洞）→**一线天**（观音石雕、定命桥、风洞、神仙楼阁）

武夷岩茶，誉满天下，正所谓"名山出名茶，名茶耀名山"。大红袍母树不可错过，300多岁的古茶树不仅仅显示着时光的印记，还承载着"半壁江山"这样的过往辉煌。爬过好汉坡的小山岗，沿着山路行至流香洞，可在溪水边席地而坐，茶会雅集随手拈来。饮茶小憩后，继续前行，可抵达慧苑寺，三教合一的老建筑以及制茶坊旧址带着烟火气和人情味。继续前行至天车架，细细端详这体现先人智慧的古崖居之后，可至天心永乐禅寺乘坐观光车，转至溪南，寻找武夷山的另一种美。

点评：

1. 该线路会经过一部分武夷岩茶核心产区，不仅可以充分领略武夷岩茶的风土之美，还能看到古茶厂的遗迹。
2. 将武夷山溪南的风景囊括进来，可体验其与九曲溪的不同之处。

◎ 神仙楼阁。（郑友裕 摄）

Gods Pavilion. (Photo by Zheng Youyu)

Option 2: Rock Bone and Flower Fragrance Wandering Path (Mother Trees of Dahongpao→Liuxiang Ravine→Huiyuan Temple→Tianche Frame)→Tianxin Yongle Zen Temple→Tiger Roaring Rock (Tiger Roaring Sights: Bailian Ferry, Jiyun Pass, Poxian Dai, Pumen Dou, Fayu Hanging River, Yu'er Spring, Bulang Boat and Binxi Cave)→A Sliver of Sky (Guanyin stone statue, Dingming Bridge, Wind Cave, and Gods Pavilion)

Wuyi Rock Tea is famous all over the world. This famous mountain is famous for its tea, and the famous tea also makes the mountain famous. The mother tea trees of Dahongpao at Jiulongke are a must-see. The three ancient trees among them are more than 300 years old, which not only show the passage of time, but also bear the glory of "half of the country". Continue your journey past the Haohan Slope and go along the mountain pathway to Liuxiang Ravine. You can sit on the ground by the stream and have a tea party there. After enjoying the tea break, walk to Huiyuan Temple, an ancient building reflecting three religions, and also the former site of a tea-making workshop. When you arrive at Tianche Frame, look carefully at the ancient cliff dwelling which embodies the wisdom of the ancient mountain people. And then take the tour bus at Tianxin Yongle Zen Temple to the south of the stream, where you can find another dimension of the beauty of Mount Wuyi.

Comments:

1. The tea plantations you pass by are part of the core region of Wuyi Rock Tea. You can fully experience the beauty of the natural conditions, the folk customs for manufacturing Wuyi Rock Tea, and see the relics of ancient tea factories.

2. This tour includes the scenery on the south of Nine-Bend Stream of Mount Wuyi, where you can notice different landscapes.

© 俯瞰慧苑禅寺。（宋春 摄）
Overlooking Huiyuan Temple. (Photo by Song Chun)

深度游主题线路

朱子理学朝圣之旅

线路1： 九曲溪竹筏漂流（六曲响声岩）→**武夷宫**→天游峰（水云寮、叔圭精舍、幼溪草庐）→**武夷精舍**

线路2： 五夫镇→朱子巷→兴贤古街→兴贤书院→朱子社仓→紫阳楼→万亩荷塘

点评：

1. 朱熹的一生除"仕宦九载，立朝四十六天"外，有半个世纪是在武夷山中度过的，留下的遗迹众多。于山水之中追寻朱子理学遗迹，体验东方理学之光，行程中涵盖书院文化，有助于深入了解儒家理论及其与日常融合的灵活教学形式。

2. 朱熹论咏武夷山的诗文甚多，其中《九曲棹歌》最为精彩。舟行溪上，一路可对照诗文，观山品水，赏心悦目。

3. 朱子故居之旅亦是朝圣之旅。五夫镇保留着一些古代特别是宋代时期的建筑，古风遗韵，千岁一日，民风亦是古朴淳厚。若是六七月间来此，正是"接天莲叶无穷碧，映日荷花别样红"，风起荷舞，美不胜收。

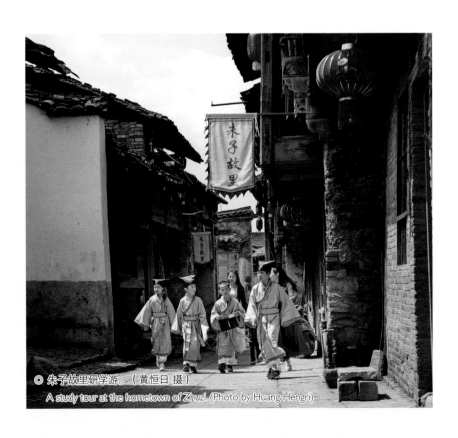

◎ **朱子故里研学游。**（黄恒日 摄）
A study tour at the hometown of Zhuzi. (Photo by Huang Hengri)

In-Depth Theme Tours

A Journey of Zhuzi's Neo-Confucianism

Option 1: Nine-Bend Stream Rafting (Xiangsheng Rock at sixth bend)→Wuyi Palace→Tianyou Peak (Shuiyun Hut, Shugui Academy, Youxi Thatched Cottage)→Wuyi Academy

Option 2: Wufu Town→Zhuzi Lane→Xingxian Ancient Street→Xingxian Academy→Zhuzi Charitable Granary→Ziyang Building →Thousands of Acres of Lotus Pond

Comments:

1. Except for "nine years of official service, and 46 days of going to court", Zhu Xi spent half a century at Mount Wuyi in his life where he left many mementoes. Follow in the footsteps of the great philosopher through the landscapes, and you may find illumination in his Neo-Confucianism. The trip covers the culture of Zhuxi's teaching academies and provides a deeper understanding of neo-Confucian theory and how its flexible teaching integrated with Chinese daily life.

2. Among Zhu Xi's many poems that praise Mount Wuyi, the most wonderful one is the *Nine-Bend Rowing Song*. Rowing on the stream, you can compare the Song with the actual landscape that you see throughout the journey.

3. This is a trip to Zhu Xi's former residence and to learn a little about his own life's journey. Wufu Town retains some ancient buildings, including those from the Song Dynasty. You can experience the thousand-year-old customs and enjoy close contact with the kind local villagers. If you go there in June or July, it's the time when the lotus blossoms are in full bloom. Watch the lotus flowers dance with the wind. It's really very beautiful and moving!

◎ 今日紫阳楼。（宋春 摄）
Today's Ziyang Building.
(Photo by Song Chun)

武夷茶岩韵之旅

线路1： 岩骨花香慢游道（大红袍母树→流香洞→慧苑寺→天车架）→**水帘洞**→**三坑两涧核心产区**（马头岩、悟源涧、九龙窠、天心岩、牛栏坑、倒水坑等）

线路2： 下梅古村落（万里茶路起点）

点评：

1. 从山场的风土、茶树品种到古茶厂遗址，完整而深入地体验武夷岩茶的"岩韵"之谜。

2. 在慧苑寺、磊石道观等处观赏三教合一老建筑的同时，可访茶问道，修身养性。幸运的话，还有可能遇到白鹇鸟哦，李白很喜欢白鹇，曾经用"夜栖寒月静，朝步落花闲"赞美它们。

3. 下梅村作为万里茶路的起点，依然保留着古民居的真实生活场景；村中"三雕"（砖雕、石雕、木雕）精美绝伦，是传统古建筑装饰当中的一朵奇葩。

◎ 下梅万里茶路起点石碑。（郑友裕 摄）

A stele inscribed with "The starting point of ten-thousand-li tea road" at Xiamei. (Photo by Zheng Youyu)

A Journey of Wuyi Rock Tea Fragrance

Option 1: Rock Bone and Flower Fragrance Wandering Path (Mother Trees of Dahongpao→ Liuxiang Ravine→Huiyuan Temple→Tianche Frame)→Water Curtain Cave→Three-Pit and Two-Ravine Core Production Area (Horse Head Rock, Wuyuan Ravine, Jiulongke, Tianxin Rock, Niulan Pit, Daoshui Pit and more)

Option 2: Xiamei Ancient Village (the starting point of thousands-li tea road)

Comments:

1. You can experience the grandeur of Wuyi Rock Tea completely and deeply from observing the tea plantation eco-conditions, learning about the different varieties of tea trees in the mountain fields, and visiting the ruins of an ancient tea factory … and enjoying the special fragrance of Wuyi Rock Tea.

2. You can also enjoy the sight of old buildings reflecting the combination of China's three historic religions in Huiyuan Temple and Leishi Taoist Temple. In the meantime you can drink tea and talk about Taoism, Buddhism and Neo-Confucianism with priests and monks there to cultivate your spirit. If you are lucky, you may see some silver pheasant birds. The famous poet, Li Bai, liked this bird very much, and wrote an elegant poem to praise them "perching quietly at night under the cold moon, dancing among the falling flowers after sunrise".

3. You can explore Xiamei Ancient Village which is the origin of the long historic tea road, viewing real scenes of ancient life and dwellings. The brick, stone and wood carvings there are very exquisite, which is regarded as the art treasure among ancient architectural ornaments.

文化与自然"双世遗"之旅

线路1： **桐木关自然保护区**（桐木关→教堂→博物馆→正山小种发源地）

线路2： 古汉城遗址→遇林亭窑址→莲花峰

点评：

1. 涵盖武夷山另外两个世遗核心区域——武夷山国家级自然保护区和武夷山古汉城遗址，可体验"双世遗"地层次丰富的自然与文化。
2. 涉猎区域广泛，最好提前做好功课，此外需要合理分配体力与时间。
3. 适宜季节为秋季。

◎ 闽越王城博物馆。（郑友裕 摄）

Minyue Kingdom Museum. (Photo by Zheng Youyu)

A Journey of Cultural and Natural Heritage

Option 1: Tongmuguan Nature Reserve (Tongmu Gateway→Church→Museum→The Birthplace of Lapsang Souchong)

Option 2: Remains of the Ancient City from the Han Dynasty→Yulin Pavilion, Site of the Song Dynasty Dragon Pottery Kiln→Lianhua Peak

Comments:

1. This is a cultural and natural journey in which you can experience other dimensions of Mount Wuyi, including the nature reserve and remains of the ancient city from the Han Dynasty.

2. It covers a large area, so you should prepare in advance—conserve your energy and allocate your time accordingly.

3. The best season to travel is in the autumn.

◎ 1924年在多米尼加铸造并运抵桐木村教堂的铜钟。（郑友裕 摄）

The bronze bell cast in Dominica and shipped to the church in Tongmu Village in 1924. (Photo by Zheng Youyu)

索 引

Index